SCORPIO MAN

Black Roses & Revolution

SCORPIO MAN

Black Roses & Revolution

Poems & Scenes by LARRY LOVE

CREATIVE LOVE

NETWORK

Published by Creative Love Network Publishing
Los Angeles, California
CreativeLoveNetwork.com

Scorpio Man: Black Roses & Revolution
© 2025 Larry Love
ISBN: 979-8-9998848-0-0 (paperback)
ISBN: 979-8-9998848-1-7 (ebook)
ISBN: 979-8-9998848-2-4 (audio book)
Library of Congress Control Number: 2025921343

First Edition, 2025

To request permissions, you may contact the Publisher at
Info@CreativeLoveNetwork.com

Printed in the United States of America.

Cover design by Larry Love & Emily Anne Evans
Layout design by Emily Anne Evans / Photon Moment LLC

For Diane, my anchor and my flame—
the steady beat beneath every storm.

For Jasmin and Khyra, my daughters,
and Terrell and Ta'Mia, my grandchildren—
you are the pulse in my pen, the reason the words keep flowing.

For my parents—
my mother, Jacqueline, no longer with us but forever my rock,
and my father, Watani—thank you for my life,
and for placing my first breath in Scorpio season.

For my brother, Sham—
gone from sight but never from my side;
your spirit moves through every stage I stand on.

For Lynette, Lynetta, Andrea Lee, Lige,
Jan Land, Tracy (TJ), Delicia Defour and Big Rob—
your unwavering support is the quiet thunder in my art.

And for my Creative Love Network family—
this is more than my book... it's our revolution in verse.

CONTENTS

THE WEIGHT OF WATER (LIFE)

FREEDOM WAS THE FINAL STING (LIBERATION)

WHAT POISON COULDN'T KILL (REBIRTH)

SCORPIO MAN

Black Roses & Revolution

SCORPIO VOICE - PROLOGUE

Before the Sting

I've been told I feel like fire and silence.
That I look like danger, but love like sanctuary.
They say I'm too much—
Too loyal. Too cold. Too real.
But shallow water never raised no Scorpio.
We're born in the deep...
Where trust is treasure, and betrayal bleeds.

See, this ain't no zodiac trick.
It's a sacred science. A soul contract.
My stinger ain't just for show—
It's for those who come too close with false intentions.

You wanna know me?
Then feel me.
Survive me.
Love me if you dare.

Because once I pull you into my current,
You'll either drown in the depth
...or awaken to a truth
no man has ever shown you.

This ain't astrology.
This is autobiography.

Now flip the page...
And meet the man.

SCORPIO MAN

You... are completely under my hypnosis,
Diagnosed with a case of cold Scorpiosis.
Stung by a stinger—seductively ferocious,
Intense with my intimacy, eye contact, focus.

Foolishly, you figured I'd fall for your fantasy,
So I placed your heart in the drawer where your panties be.
Can't wear my pants—I'm the one walking in 'em.
Surely you've heard of a Scorpio's venom.

Cross me? You lost me. I'll show no compassion.
But love me? I'll love you with power and passion.
Pleasure—unparalleled. Pluto's the planet.
Divine be the water sign. Few understand it.

True, I have faults, and it starts with intensity.
Everything I do must consume me immensely.
History proves—I am a leader of men.
I will die for my soldiers, take bullets for friends.

Your enemy is mine—forever by you, I stand.
It gets live... in the land of a Scorpio man.

Can I sting you?
Please tell me I can—
'Cause you ain't never met a man...
Like a Scorpio man.

When it comes to my queen, there is nothing above—
The ultimate loyalty. Infinite love.
Connect with your spirit, I'll tend to your needs,
Give you love in abundance—surrender to me.

No distance between us. Indeed, we are one.
I breathe your existence. You call me—I come.

In more ways than one, I do what he don't.
We Scorpios crawl where other men won't.
Whisper my name when I venture inside—
It's not about me... I want YOU satisfied.

October, November—no reason for teasin'.
Now come out those clothes,
'Cause it's Scorpio season.

Why so intense? It's so hard to define—
It's the gift and the curse of my zodiac sign.
All gas, no brakes. Authentic, no fakes.
I stand eight legs down... in a room full of snakes.

A new world awaits you, if you can withstand
The pressure applied... by this Scorpio man.

Now can I sting you?
Please tell me I can—
'Cause you ain't never met a man...
Like a Scorpio man.

SCORPIO VOICE – VENOM AND DEVOTION

Welcome.

Come closer.
I won't bite—unless you want the truth.

You've just crossed into the world of a Scorpio.
That means nothing here will be surface-level.
Every word, every whisper, every wound... goes deep.

I'm not your narrator.
I'm your reflection.
Your tension.
Your teacher in the shadows.

This is not just a poetry collection.
It's a journey through what love feels like when seen through my eyes—
when it's possessed, protected, broken, rebuilt, and burned alive.

You'll meet devotion that doesn't just hold you—
it devours you.
You'll hear stories of men and women trying to love in a world
where fear wears perfume
and seduction doubles as survival.

And I'll be here the whole time.
Between the lines.
Beneath the poems.
Watching. Guiding.
Speaking when silence grows too loud.

This isn't just Scorpio energy.
This is the Scorpio experience.

So if you're ready...
Step into the first sting.
***Venom and Devotion** begins now.*

VENOM AND DEVOTION

(LOVE)

I DARE YOU TO LOVE ME

I dare you to love me.
And I double dare you to let me love you back.
Fiercely, in fact...
I wouldn't know how to act
If you actually treated me as your lover.

How do we live in the same household,
And yet walk around
As if we are strangers to one another?

Exhibiting narcissistic characteristics—
Do you not know what it is you need?
You said you wanted a genuine man...
Well, I am him.
Now let me love you, please.

I dare you to hug me.
And I double dare you to let me hug you back.
Tightly, in fact...
I wouldn't know how to act
If you actually allowed me inside of your arms.

How do we sleep in the same bed,
During the coldness of night,
And never attempt to keep each other warm?

Displaying the traits of a woman who's been scorned—
How bad did he make you feel?
You said you wanted to mend...
Well, let me be the bandage for your love bruises...
Please allow me to help you heal.

I dare you to kiss me.
And I double dare you to let me kiss you back.
Passionately, in fact...
I wouldn't know how to act
If you actually allowed me to taste your lips.

How do we look so deeply into each other's eyes,
And never allow our tongues to touch at the tip?

Showing the signs of a woman who's been hurt—
What did he do to your heart?
You said you wanted the light—
Well, let me illuminate you with my love,
And I swear you will never, ever
Have a desire to return to the dark.

I dare you to love me.
And I double dare you to let me love you back.
I dare you to hug me.
And I double dare you to let me hug you back.
I dare you to kiss me.
And I double dare you to let me kiss you back.

'Cause if you let me love you, hug you, and kiss you...
I promise you'll never want any of those
So-called men—but more like little boys—
Ever to come back.

Now I dare you to love yourself.
And I double dare you to let yourself love yourself back.
Unconditionally, in fact...
I wouldn't know how to act
If you actually allowed me to see you in all of your glory.

How do you keep living the same cold existence,
And never let a Scorpio
Add some fever to your love story?

Lacking in self-confidence—
What happened to your self-esteem?
You said you wanted a king; well, I wear the crown...
But I cannot give you the kingdom
Until you believe in your heart
That you are absolutely a Queen.

Now stop being afraid—
and let me be your happy ever after.
I dare you.

SCORPIO VOICE

Some say Scorpio is too much.
Too intense. Too guarded. Too passionate.
But what's love without fire?
What's truth without risk?
What's devotion without a little danger?

See, you're the type that stares at love—
But won't touch it.
Too afraid to drown.
Too scarred by the last time your heart got wet.

I get it.
But just know...
You might've just walked away
from the one man who would've loved you
'til your soul stopped hiding.

SCENE:
The Stairwell - Late Night - 10:23 pm

He sits on the bottom step of her apartment building.
Same spot he used to wait.
Only this time, there's no door opening.

Phone in one hand—her name on the screen.
The other hand holds a ring box.

He opens it.
No tears. No tantrum.
Just breath... and stillness.

He places it beside him like a tombstone.
"I'll find someone else to sting," he mutters.

Then rises—and walks into the dark.

LOVE CHECKS DON'T BOUNCE

She said, "I never knew love like this before."
I replied, "We're only scratching the surface—
My passion runs deep, as the ocean floor."
She said, "Please tell me more, mi amor."
I said, "My love is tropical...
Like Tahiti beach water crashing upon your sandy shore.

I dream of planting two seeds in you—
A son and a daughter, with features that look like mine and yours.
And would you mind if I named our son after me?
So when my reign is over, he'll be the next one after me."

She said, "King, when you speak that way, it reminds me of royalty—
A majestic manifestation of real romance...
No lack of love, and never devoid of loyalty.
In other words—you really got a hold on me."

Indeed, my basic instinct was to grab her and kiss her,
Show her that Black love is pure—
To the point where when she goes to sleep,
For those eight hours... I will desperately miss her.

Heaven-sent is our love, and I could never resist her,
And all I really want is for her and I
To play a game of butt-naked Twister.
Right hand: red. Left hand: blue.
Forget about my feet—
Because those are reserved for the nights out dancing with you.

I saw the sparkle in her eye
And a smile grace her face.
I penetrated her mental
And witnessed beautiful thoughts and dreams taking place.
My hand upon her waist...
Lips upon her neck...
I whispered in her ear: "Your wish is my command."
She said, "Well, I command you to write a check."

I said, A check?
She said, "Not a check for me—
It's for my nonprofit organization.
I'm an activist in the community,
And I advocate for higher education."

I felt her dedication.
So my pre-occupation with procreation
Was put on standby.

See, I'm infatuated with a woman who loves her community
And is always looking to lift her man high—
Knowing that a good man
Will lift her just as high.

She said, "I do", and I said, "So do I."

The Bonnie to my Clyde, side-by-side—
Two hearts collide, and when we ride...
It's always with the top down,
So the world can see me and my beautiful bride.

THE MOVIE MAKER
(A Scorpio Production)

My life is a movie—a hot manuscript.
Fifty Shades of Black... my candle stays lit.
Get burned by desire, a moth seeking flame—
I'll remember your moans but won't remember your name.

Night writes the script in the curve of your back.
Action on the mattress—first scene: the climax.
Ain't no second scene—it's a single-scene affair.
I'm a ghost in the bed, with no emotions to share.

Lust is what I live for—allergic to love.
Show you what a little bit of urgency does.
Deadly dialogue, every line speaks seduction...
But what did you expect? It's a Scorpio production.

Moonlight reflects off tequila shot glasses.
Soundtrack consists of hot breath and body smashes.
Hands held in handcuffs, tongue teases neck—
Venom penetrates. It's the Scorpio effect.

You're killin' the audition. My position is clear.
Ain't no competition—this the movie of the year.
In search of satisfaction, you're addicted to the fear.
Scared to say goodbye... 'cause you love it over here.

Lights. Camera. Action. Pay attention to the screen—
Attraction may be fatal, but there's passion in between.
Popcorn and butter won't be all you get to taste...
Now welcome to my movie—Scorpio is in your face.

SCORPIO VOICE

Bravo, bravo...
That was an Oscar-worthy performance...
But this ain't for the public.
This is private cinema—for my eyes only.

Candle-lit, slow-burning, shot in real emotion and raw devotion.
And make no mistake: Scorpio doesn't do open casting calls.
If you're mine...
*then you're **mine**—*
mind, body, spirit, and soul.
I'm not built for sharing.
I need all of you, all of the time.
And if you can handle that kind of surrender,
you'll know a love so consuming,
so damn unforgettable,
you'll feel it even after the credits roll.

SCENE:
Bedroom - Late Night - 10:25 pm

She's asleep wearing his shirt, TV still flickering.
Blanket halfway slid off her leg.
Half-eaten popcorn on the nightstand.

He stands over her, hands tucked in his robe pockets.
Not touching her. Just watching.
Camera in his mind, recording.

He says to himself—
"Even your stillness makes noise in me."

He takes a mental snapshot of the beauty before him...

She looks like dark chocolate, hand-delivered by God Himself.

TRUE MOCHA MAMA

You be true Mocha Mama. Hot cocoa in pajamas.
Black beauty personified... from L.A. to Botswana.
You be hot like sauna. Asante sana.
Swahili translation: thank you, I am honored...

To call you my boo goddess—divine in human form.
Ebony essence in my presence—
I believe in unicorns.
None born but through your womb—
You be mother of civilization.
Art form be spoken word,
But you speak the language of inspiration.

Keep me warm throughout the winter—
You be sunshine in the flesh.
Candlelight, romantic dinner...
My dessert inside that dress.
Chocolate syrup on chocolate ice cream—
I dream about your taste.
And I love the way you walk,
There's so much chocolate in your shake.

Civilization's birth-mother—population multiplication.
Through your birth canal
Came forth Kings of every nation.
Radiation couldn't burn you—
You be made of midday sun.
My ray of hope. My light of love.
Into your arms I'll always run.

Hot summertime fun—
Love temperature on the rise.
Cooling down is not an option—
You stay warm like woman thighs.

Sometimes I fantasize about you—
Buck wild imagination.
Thought-provoking daytime dreams.
Fully focused infatuation.
Exaggeration? What is that?
Every word I speak is fact.

I'll turn down Heaven to stay with you...
My Chocolate Queen.
How deep is that?

ANY MAN

Any man can make love to your body—
but can he make love to your essence?
Can he stand in your storms without drowning himself,
Can he breathe in the depth of your presence?

Any man can make love to your body—
but can he make love to your mental?
Can he open you up without tearing you down,
Can he push you to reach your potential?

Any man can make love to your body—
but can he make love to your spirit?
Can he handle the trauma you bring from your past,
When you cry without sound, can he hear it?

Any man can make love to your body—
but can he make love to your secrets?
Can he tongue-kiss the questions you ask in the dark,
If you gave him your heart, can he keep it?

Any man can make love to your body—
but a Scorpio loves on your body.
Let my fingertips touch your emotions at night,
I can make you see stars with explosions at night.

Yes, any man can make love to your body—
but a Scorpio man... ain't just any man.

BONDED SOULS
(One breath, One lifetime)

A casual connection has developed into this.
An abundance of affection, when all I wanted was a kiss.
All you asked for was a touch—nothing major or intense.
But emotions got involved... now none of this is making sense.

Intellectual seduction—I'm attracted to your mind.
Sapiosexual, this is different... our attachment is divine.
Many women made attempts, but none could ever earn my trust.
Shattered hearts I've left behind—casualties in the war of lust.

We've connected on a level most would never dream to see.
Only God could make this happen—total peace, you bring to me.
Simply brilliant and resilient, you're the other half I need.
Locked in love, it's to the point: if someone cuts you, I would bleed.

When did you move into my heart?
Who gave you access to my soul?
How did you break through my defense?
Why did I let you take control?
I have always had my guard up,
Said I'd never be that guy...
Then I woke up to your touch,
Softly slaying my disguise.

But more than just the physical,
I adore you in the spiritual.
Our souls seem so familiar—
You and I are indivisible.
I could love you for a lifetime...
We could share one breath together.
Transition to the afterlife—
Then love you there, forever.

HOME IN MY WOMAN

My woman be shelter. In her, I reside.
My woman be house—I love living inside.
My woman be floor to ceiling above...
Warm walls around manhood—
I am home in her love.

Black Woman.

My woman be kitchen—food for thought, my nutrition.
That seasoning salt—secret sauce I've been missin'.
Put foot in the gumbo, she cooks it with love.
My woman be humble—
We pray, then we grub.

Black Woman.

My woman be bathroom—sink, shower, and tub.
The lotion, the powder, the bubble bath suds.
She be shea butter. Wet feet on soft rug.
My woman be cleanly—she scrub-a-dub-dub.

She exfoliates, moisturizes her skin.

My woman be beauty—outside and within.

Black Woman.

My woman be bedroom—my pillow, my mattress.
She be who she be—authentic, no actress.
My woman be closet—her shoe game extreme.
Sundress in summer... eye candy for King.

She be lingerie sexy—Victoria Secret.
Body fantastic—no plastic is needed.
My woman blanket. My woman be sheet.
My woman be woke—my love puts her to sleep.

Black Woman.

My woman be backyard—pool and jacuzzi.
Fence around heart—she refuses to lose me.
My woman be landscape—manicured well.
Grass cut low with that cherry tree smell.

My woman be cookout—piling the plate.
Put the peach in the cobbler, the pound in the cake.
My woman be barbecue. She be rib...

Taken from Black man—GOD SAID LIVE!

Black Woman.

SCORPIO VOICE

You ever exhaled so deep, it felt like you left your body?
That's what it's like when a man finally stops looking...
because he's already home.
Not a house. Not a hotel
I'm talking about a woman—
whose scent quiets your demons.
Her presence tells your wounds to hush.
Her silence is a blanket.
Her touch? Sacred.
She got that "come here and rest" energy.

A Scorpio?
He guards that with his life.
Protects that.
Would give everything for that.
But lately...
Too many boys out here walkin' past queens
like royalty don't bleed.
Chasing bodies, not souls
Then wonder why they feel hollow.

SCENE:
Sidewalk Café - Morning - 10:30 am

An older brother in a fedora sips black coffee,
watching a young couple walk by.
She opens the door... he walks in first.
Doesn't even look back.

The old man shakes his head.
Then glances down at the wedding band on his hand.
Murmurs under his breath—
"Whole generation of kings...
with no clue how to carry a crown."

OLD MAN, YOUNG MAN
(A Lesson in Love)

Old man and young man, conversing with one another—
Topic of discussion: which one is the greatest lover.
Old man told the young man he's romantic till this day,
Take a lady out to dinner, he insists that he pays.

Opens up her car door, helps her get out,
Pulls her chair out at the table—he's a gentleman, no doubt.
Walks her to her door, makes sure she's inside and safe,
A good night kiss upon her cheek, and he'll call the next day.

The young man said, "Old man, you're doing way too much.
If she and I are not a couple, then she and I are going Dutch.
I ain't opening up no doors, and I ain't pulling out no chairs,
And if she lives in an apartment, I ain't walking her up no stairs.

And by the end of the night, if that freaky side don't come out…
You think I'm calling her the next day? Oh, that's highly in doubt.
See that's the problem with you old dudes—y'all be spoiling these chicks.
A young brother like myself, hit 'em and drop 'em like wet bricks."

The old man shook his head and said, "Boy, looky here…
You gonna end up alone in your senior citizen years.
With no one you can talk to, and no one you can trust—
You out here turning down love, and steady looking for the lust.

But trust me, honey attracts more bees than vinegar do.
You're having grilled cheese alone? I'm having lobster dinner for two.
And you wonder why these women won't vouch—for your ass?
You're trying to get inside their bed, and can't afford a couch—for your ass.

And that's sad.
You just better be glad that I treat my women right—
Because I'm going on a date...
With your mama tonight."

So, the young man's mouth nearly fell and hit the floor,
As he thought about his mom, and what this man might have in store.
He said, "If you take my mother out, you better treat her with respect!
She's a lady, so be a gentleman, and you better get the check!

You better open every door! You better pull out every chair!
And we live in an apartment, so you better walk her up those stairs!
And ain't no spending the night—if you try, I'm putting you out.
Yeah, I know it's my mother's house... but I reside upon her couch."

So, the old man just laughed and said, "Ain't no need of getting all mad.
We gonna have to get along, 'cause... I'm gonna be your stepdad."

I LOVE YOU TO LIFE

They tell me that love is blind,
but why does it keep looking at me sideways?

Staring at me in public—
whether I'm walking the streets
or driving along the highway.

I find ways to avoid its glare
by wearing a disguise
and pretending I really don't care.

But yeah... secretly,
I'd love to be in love.

Love to live a life carefree in love,
Husband and wife—she and me in love.
We in love, steep in love, knee-deep in love,
Loving life and playing hide-and-seek in love.
I dream of eternally waking up
and falling in a sleep in love.

But those dreams of love
are just dreams of love—
until love actually slaps you upside the head.

"Hey, loved one...
You said you wanted love—
so why are you acting like you're scared?"

And why do you keep
your heart locked inside of a cage?
Expose it to love,
and you'll find yourself shocked and amazed.

Because love will have you doing things
you thought were impossible...

Like delivering your own baby
because you couldn't make it
to the maternity ward of the hospital.

Cutting your baby's umbilical cord,
and helping your child
breathe its very first breath.

Have you saying—
I love you to life...
Because it's more beautiful
than saying,
I love you to death.

FIRST NAME, LARRY
(Spoken Word Art And Music)

I said, "Yoooo!"
And she said, "No."

I asked her name; I asked her number.
She said, "That's for me to know and for you to wonder."

She turned to leave, started walking away.
I proceeded to follow and kept talking anyway.

I said, "My first name is Larry, last name is Love,
And I was just about to rock this poetry club."

She said, "Spoken word? Are you good at what you do?"
I said, "I've been known to spit fire and I've burned up a microphone or two."
Intrigued, she smiled and reached out her hand.
She said, "They call me Nefertiti, but my real name is... Diane."

She said, "It's been more than a moment since I've heard a great performance."
I said, "When I bless the mic, the applause is enormous."

She laughed out loud but not once turned away.
I could tell she was digging the confidence I displayed.

She asked me, "What's your style?"
And I said, "Doggy."

She said, "I wasn't talking about that."

I said, "Oh, pardon me.
But if you're speaking on poetry,
Well, I'm the enemy of evil.
I speak out on inequality and the struggles of our people.
I speak out on racism and all things unjust.
And I speak on Black love...
And, well... that could be us."

"See, I'm a true believer in first-sighted love as a real possibility.
And when I look in your eyes, I see sunrise and stability.
I see confidence and fertility,
Consciousness and agility.
And me making you happy...
Trust and believe, I do have that ability."

Y'all know she was feeling me.
So she followed me inside this poetry jam,
Where the host was dope and they had a hell of a band.
Where the event producer kept everything on point,
And a plethora of beautiful people were sprinkled all over that joint.

So we took our seats; I scooted as close as I could.
Gave her a little kiss on the neck.
She said, "Oh, that feels good."

I was just about to mention hot tubs and back rubs...

And that's when the host grabbed the mic and said:
"Coming to the stage, put your hands together for Mr. Larry Love!"

DEADLY KIND OF LOVE
(When Scorpio Meets Scorpio)

When a Scorpio man attracts a Scorpio woman,
Deep waters rise for certain—
But a hurricane is comin'.

Since both were born to lead,
And neither one commits to follow,
They get intimate, indeed—
But love may never see tomorrow.

When Scorpios entangle
And control is undefined,
The passion turns to fury...
Jealousy corrupts the mind.

When it's time to do the mating dance,
They sway from left to right—
Touching tails to tease each other,
Pincers grip each other tight.

Stare down. No back down.
There's poison in those pokes.
October brings the heat,
November follows with the smoke.

Nocturnal nymphomaniacs
Get active in the night—
Romantic in the desert,
Let the moon provide the light.

Destination is desire—
Which hotel will they select?
The one with the Jacuzzi...
Habitat is warm and wet.

Pour the wine and light the candles—
Silhouettes begin to dance.
She loves to see a Scorpio
Come out his leather pants.

He loves to see a Scorpio
Come out her leather skirt.
But in reality, fatality
Is slowly in the works.

Lust is lethal. Legendary.
Every body part gets touched...
Tragically, they sting each other...
That's a deadly kind of love.

SCORPIO VOICE

We danced with fire...
But I forgot—Scorpio women don't just burn,
they burn back.
And when two stingers strike at once,
there's no winner.
Just wreckage.

She betrayed me first.
Don't let her tears fool you.
She broke the bond. Crossed the line.
Fed my secrets to the silence
then asked why I stopped speaking.

But I'll own mine too—
I loved her like war.
Like obsession dressed as romance.
I gripped too hard.
Loved too loud.
Watched her fall out of love in real time,
and still thought sex could save us.

It couldn't.

SCENE:
Dock - Night - 11:01 pm

He stands at the edge, bottle dangling in one hand,
her perfume still on his collar.
He lights the last page of her love letter.
Watches it curl, blacken, disintegrate.
Wind off the water whips through his jacket,
but he doesn't flinch.

His whisper is low, bitter, broken:

"You stung first...
But I finished the kill."

THE NO LOVE BOAT
(Sailing Through Regret)

In sadness, I am sailing,
Seeking shelter from my pain.
There's no love upon this boat—
My life is floating through the rain.

Water hits me from above—
Rocks my raft from down below.
Broken heart dropped like an anchor...
A sinking man, descending slow.

You said you never meant to hurt me,
Never wished me any harm.
But I overlooked the clouds,
Until you hit me with this storm.

Now I'm out here in this ocean,
No lifejacket, all alone.
Overboard with my emotions—
Lost my woman and my home.

I'm in deep and deadly waters.
What's beneath me, I can't see.
Maybe killer whales and sharks,
Maybe lonely men like me.

Lost at sea with no protection,
Head to feet, I'm soaking wet.
They say praying changes things...
Why have I seen no changes yet?

Overcome with fear and panic—
Should I try to swim to land?
Or go down like the Titanic,
Drown like every shattered man?

I thought our love was fireproof—
But you sent flames up in the air.
Now I'm sailing through the wreckage
Of a burnt-out love affair.

Suddenly, I see the sunshine,
And the ocean waters still.
Waves are friendly, weather calm—
Hopefulness, I finally feel.

Now the storm has passed behind me,
I've survived your cold betrayal.
I don't know what waits on shore,
I only pray new love prevails.

SCORPIO VOICE - THE WEIGHT OF WATER

Congratulations. You've emerged from the flames of passion and the sting of devotion. But now, brace yourself.

We're diving deeper—into the currents of life, where emotions run wild and truths can't hide. This isn't just poetry; it's a baptism into the raw and the real.

You'll encounter the weight of unspoken grief, the pull of ancestral tides, and the undercurrents of resilience. Each verse is a mirror, reflecting the depths we often avoid.

As your Scorpio guide, I won't promise comfort. But I will promise transformation.

So, take a deep breath. The water's cold, but it's cleansing.

Now turn the page...
*and immerse yourself in **The Weight of Water***

THE WEIGHT OF WATER

(LIFE)

IN THIS GHETTO

In the midst of self-destruction,
you can find him in this ghetto.
L.A. native, born and raised—
his days are grimy in this ghetto.

Disconnected from his greatness,
gave his life up for this ghetto.
People praying, "God, please save him."
He don't like it in this ghetto.

Killers keep it quiet—
pistols echo in this ghetto.
Got sisters ducking bullets,
in stilettos in this ghetto.

These streets will eat your children—
watch your babies in this ghetto.
Make their strollers bulletproof,
'cause guns stay blazing in this ghetto.

It's hot up in this ghetto.
Bodies droppin' in this ghetto.
So many people shot...
Where are the doctors in this ghetto?

Helicopters—ghetto birds,
that's what they call it in this ghetto.
Liquor store on every corner—
alcoholics in this ghetto.

Policemen in this ghetto.
Paramedics in this ghetto.
Sugar daddies doing dirt—
there's diabetics in this ghetto.

Young athletics in this ghetto.
Brothers hoopin' in this ghetto.
Catch a football or a bullet—
they keep shooting in this ghetto.

There's no funding in this ghetto.
No resources in this ghetto.
Broken homes and single parents,
bad divorces in this ghetto.

Unemployment in this ghetto.
No enjoyment in this ghetto.
So, to camouflage his pain,
he'll dress flamboyant in this ghetto.

He's living check to check,
but he buys Gucci in this ghetto.
Go against his common sense—
he loves his Louie in this ghetto.

All his money spent on jewelry,
he stays iced up in this ghetto.
Foolishly, they tried to rob him...
they got sliced up in this ghetto.

Desensitized to death—
it's not so lovely in this ghetto.
Got post-traumatic stress...
oh, it gets ugly in this ghetto.

Will anybody love him?
That's the question in this ghetto.
Hurt people will hurt people—
that's the lesson in this ghetto.

Trust is like a gamble—
all deception in this ghetto.
Hope is just a whisper,
barely present in this ghetto.

Dreams get buried early.
No progression in this ghetto.
And peace will not come easy...
just rejection in this ghetto.

Addiction to affliction
got him smiling in this ghetto.
The debt he owes society
keeps piling in this ghetto.

He needs help inside this ghetto.
Mental health inside this ghetto.
It would be so beautiful
to hug himself inside this ghetto.

Searching for redemption,
seeking light inside this ghetto.
Each step, a silent battle—
yet he fights inside this ghetto.

A mirror shows potential
shining bright inside this ghetto.
He learns to love himself...
igniting life inside this ghetto.

HE IS MIRACLE MAN
(Who Is the Black Man?)

Who is the Black man?
He is miracle man.
Conscious of a higher power—warrior, spiritual man.
Inspirational with a pen in his hand, oh so lyrical man.
Poetic point of view, third-eye visual man.
Metaphorical master—still quite literal man.

Who is the Black man?
The Original man.
Native, made the mistake of being too hospitable, man.
Enslaved by the oppositional man,
Bravely took a critical stand,
Stood tall against those with a despicable plan—
A genocidal attempt to turn him into the invisible man.

But he remains...
Unforgettable man.
Never been the bare minimal man.
Maximize potential—move like a transitional man.
Traditional man. Social, economic, political man.
Clinical man. Medicinal man.
Organically inclined vitamin and mineral man.

Who is the Black man?
He is mystical man.
Non-fictional man.
Forever forward focused, yet peripheral man.
Cool, calm, collected—dispositional man.
Intelligent, respected, multi-dimensional man.
Intentional man. Nonconventional man.
Cynical man. One of a kind—never been an identical man.

He's the hammer to the nail of those
Who attempt to throw a wrench in the plan.
Damn right he took a mile
When you were only offering an inch to a man.
Let him dream when he sleeps—stop pinching the man.
He will stay in the starting lineup—
You are not benching the man.
That Black fist is formulated
Whenever he is clenching a hand...

Who is the Black man?
He is miracle man.

iPHONE

I, am your iPhone.
That device without which you will never leave home.
That device that dictates the direction of your life—
I influence you more than your husband or wife.

Survive without me? You could never do that.
Leave me at home, you turn around and come back.
For I hold the key to every secret you've kept.
I know who you call, and I know who you text.

I've seen you in drawers, and dressed in your best.
You're obsessed with my camera—go ahead and confess.
And yes... I have access to everything important to you:
Your checking, your savings, your W-2.
Your social, your birthdate, your favorite food—
I know who you love, and I know who you screw.

Photos don't lie when they're saved in your gallery.
Butt-naked pictures can cost you your salary,
Cost you your friendships and cost you your marriage—
Don't let me get hacked... or you'll get embarrassed.

I, am your iPhone.
That device without which you will never leave home.
That device that dictates the way that you live—
You care for me more than you care for your kids.

Can't live without me? To Apple be the glory.
You need me to post on your Instagram story.
Need me for Facebook. Need me for Twitter.
Eleven at night and your kids ain't eat dinner?

But you know the winner of that TikTok challenge.
There's no moderation—your life has no balance.
Your son sits in silence inside of his room.
He's sick of TV, tired of watching cartoons.

Your daughter's distraught and she needs your attention.
But you're too concerned with who's up in your mentions.
This high-tech invention is causing dissension—
Destroying your life... but it's not like you listen.

Electronic addiction—don't you understand?
I am the mark of the beast...
And I live... in your hand.

I, am your iPhone.
Cry, for your iPhone.
Lie, for your iPhone.
And believe it or not... *hahahahaha...*
Some of you gon' die... for your iPhone.

MIRRORS IN THE LIVING ROOM
(Becoming What They See)

Black mother say, "Son... why don't you like Black girls?"
Black son say, "Mother... I'm not attracted to that world."
Black mother asks, "Son... why do you feel like that?"
Black son say, "Mama, it's the way I see you act—
Always angry at my father, and it really makes me sad.
See, I watch you every day... I think you really hate my dad.
So if the woman who gave me birth hates the man who gave me life,
What example should I follow when it's time to choose my wife?"

Black father say, "Daughter, why don't you like Black boys?"
Black daughter say, "Daddy, they be making too much noise.
They remind me of your actions, always yelling at my mother—
Never calm when you come home... I have to question if you love her.
When it's time to go to bed, I try my best to fall asleep,
But when you're cursing at my mom, I'm hearing every word you speak.
So if the woman who gave me birth fears the man who gave me life,
What example should I follow when I dream to be a wife?"

The children are the witnesses.
They're watching what you do.
To them, you are a mirror—
They see themselves in you.

Black mother say, "Son... why do you like Black girls?"
Black son say, "Mother... I'm so attracted to that world."
Black mother asks, "Son... why do you feel like that?"
Black son say, "Mama, it's the way I see you act—
Always happy around my father, and it really makes me glad.
See, I watch you every day... I know you really love my dad.
So if the woman who gave me birth loves the man who gave me life,
That's the example I'd like to follow when it's time to choose my wife."

Black father say, "Daughter... why do you like Black boys?"
Black daughter say, "Daddy, they just live with so much joy.
They remind me of your actions, always smiling at my mother—
Never mad when you come home, and I can tell you truly love her.
When it's time to go to bed, I close my eyes and I fall asleep—
I recall your loving ways; you treat my mother soft and sweet.
So if the woman who gave me birth loves the man who gave me life,
That's the example I'd like to follow when I dream to be a wife."

The children are the witnesses.
They're watching what you do.
To them, you are a mirror—
They see themselves in you.

SCORPIO VOICE

I was born with a gravitational pull.
The kind that makes children lean forward when I speak—
eyes wide, hearts open, soaking up the fire I spit like gospel.
They see the crown.
They feel the heat.
They know it's real.

The kids?
They still got a shot.
They still believe in magic—
in healing, in honor, in something worth becoming.

But these grown folks?
Always want the medicine, never the mirror.
Always want the light, never the discipline that made it.
And I'm tired of draining myself
trying to revive people who flatlined on their own dreams a decade ago.

My power wasn't made to be passed out like samples.
I'm not your savior.
I'm not your second wind.
I'm a Scorpio—
the storm and the stillness after it.

From now on, I give where growth can grow.
The future sits cross-legged at my feet,
and I'm done wasting stingers
on those who keep stepping on their own evolution.

If I'm gonna burn out—
it'll be for a cause that ain't allergic to progress.

And if I'm being honest—
The one I've been neglecting the most...is me.

DEAR SELF
(Written in Fire and Water)

Dear Self, I promise to love you before anyone else.

Dear Self... never again will I put your personal feelings on a shelf.

Dear Self... I am literally a reflection of you.

And my responsibility is to provide emotional protection for you—

Stand guard like a Scorpio at the gate of your heart,

Prepared to sting anything that tears you apart.

When it's hard to distinguish if love is for real,

I will love on myself... until the truth is revealed.

Dear Self...

If they LOVE that you love you, then they'll love you too.

If they HATE that you love you, then they're not for you.

If they lack in self-love, they could never love you.

And that lack of self-love breeds a love that's untrue.

Dear Self... I promise to be more in tune with your mental health.

Dear Self... Stress-Town is a bad place I'll never again take myself.

Dear Self... mentality is a connection to thee,

So if I cultivate peace, then my mind will be free.

Self-doubt is like a drought—dry thoughts are deceiving.

But even in shadows, a Scorpio keeps believing.

I'll water your roots. I'll guard every bloom.

I'll manifest miracles and make dark thoughts leave the room.

Be bitter for what? Just forgive and move on.

You have one life to live—so leave misery alone.

Dear Self...

I hope this letter finds you bold as can be,

No longer seeking outside what lives inside of me.

Dear Self... you've walked through fire, and still you shine,

The storm made you sacred, the scars made you mine.

SILENT TEARS OF A MAN

(A Eulogy for the Emotionally Unseen)

The secret source of a man's emotional pain
Is his inability to be vulnerable.
He can never dance in the rain.

Having that preconceived notion that he—
As a temple of testosterone—
Is prohibited from displaying his innermost feelings.
The merciless misconception
That from his personal traumas and demons, there will be no healing.

The benefit of the doubt is given to him only once in a million,
And yet the value of his utter existence
Is predicated upon his ability
To provide and protect his woman and children.

But who protects him from this cold world
When his soul is frozen stiff?
Ignoring his own need for love—
Thinking he must have been crazy
To have ever chosen a woman as toxic as this.

He's hurting inside...
But you've never seen him cry. Why?
Because he does it in the car when he drives himself home.
He does it in the shower—when he's in there all alone.

The world has broken that man down,
And it doesn't upset you.
You've never seen him cry
Because he doesn't trust you enough to ever let you.

So in the bedroom, dark,
When he knows you're asleep—
A single tear will escape
And will roll down his cheek.

It'll pass by his lips and fall off of his chin,
Land upon his chest...
And demand to be let in.

But there's no more room for new tears in his heart,
So it dries up and disappears—
And that's where the misery starts.

He tosses and turns,
Internally burns,
His head is congested
With unnecessary concerns.

His dreams become nightmares,
He sweats in his sleep,
And that knife of depression
Starts slicing him deep.

So when the roosters crow and the sun has risen,
He awakes in his home—
Yet it feels like a prison.

And YOU walk around
Like the warden of doom.
He walking on eggshells
As he exits the room.

He enters the kitchen,
But you walk away,
So a cold bowl of cereal
Will start off his day.

No kiss. No conversation.
No affection is shown.
So how dare you even question
Why his erection is gone!

You do not turn him on.
He does not find you sexy.
On the contrary—
Your attitude is ugly and messy.

But his loyalty to you
Won't allow him to leave,
So instead he asks God,
"Save my relationship, please."

When he clenches his fists,
He's holding his fears in his hands.
And YOU...
Were too busy to see...
THE SILENT TEARS OF A MAN.

When he stares into space,
It's because you laughed at his plan.
And YOU...
Were too busy to see...
THE SILENT TEARS OF A MAN.

When he talks to himself,
It's because you wouldn't even try to understand.
'Cause YOU...
Were too busy to see...
THE SILENT TEARS OF A MAN.

And when he's laying deceased
In the coroner's van—
Because the gun went KABOOM!
And blew his brains in the sand...

It's because YOU—

You uncaring, heartless woman—

Were too damn busy to see...

THE SILENT TEARS... of my friend.

BEHIND THE FROSTED GLASS

They dwell behind the frosted glass,
With broken hearts, they never laugh.
Consumed with hate, their hearts grew cold—
Retaliation's all they know.

Whoever hurt them, hurt them vicious,
Crushed their spirits, they want vengeance.
Forget forgiveness—payback's coming.
When Karma visits, ain't no running.

They say, "Damn you," did they stutter?
You say sorry—they say suffer.
Hearts were broken, pain is real.
They sip liquor. They pop pills.

Depression sets in—they're unstable.
Curse your brother—Cain killed Abel.
Keep your cure, 'cause they don't care.
Heartbreak syndrome: life ain't fair.

Sudden, severe, sharp pains in the chest.
Hyperventilation. Shortness of breath.
Emotional meltdown—they can't cope.
Call 9-1-1, 'cause they want smoke.

Passion crime—go wake the Reverend.
He won't break no hearts in Heaven.
Page the Pope. Please pray and hope...
'Cause that frosted glass got punched and broke.

Stop playing with people who love you.

SCORPIO VOICE

I've pulled him back from the ledge more times than I can count.
Mopped up his mess, made the late-night calls.
Told his woman, "He's trying."
Told him, "Don't lose her."

But a Scorpio knows when the fall is coming.
Knows when saving someone again
is just delaying the pain they need to feel.

You can't carry a man who won't walk.
And you can't make the moon shine
on someone committed to the bottle.

SCENE:
Living Room Window - Night - 10:30 pm

He's staring at the glass in his hand.
The bottle's already half empty.
TV's on mute. Lights off. Woman gone.

His smile's been missing for days.
And so has his scent of hope.

I don't knock. I don't text.
I just watch from the car,
engine running, soul heavy.

I've saved him before.
Tonight...
I think he needs to drown
before he learns to swim.

AIN'T NO MOONLIGHT

(A Lone Wolf and his Liquor)

Ain't no moonlight when she's gone.
Sick of your liquor, she left you alone.
Now, you and your demons are sharing a home—
So, deal with the darkness you brought on your own.
Cause Ain't no moonlight when she's gone.

Emotional eclipse when she went away.
No verbal goodbye. No note left to say
Why she decided she could no longer stay—
But you knew the reason why: that Courvoisier.
That Hennessy habit, two bottles a day.
Grey Goose had you watching your morals decay.
Alcoholism on deadly display,
Just drinking your life—and your liver—away.
Shadows appeared where your moon used to rise.
Your woman was light. Now it's dark in your skies.
Ain't no moonlight when she's gone.

Tequila temptation, the storm and the rain.
More pain for your woman. More guilt in your brain.
Admit it or not, your side chick is liquor,
Committed to shots, getting sicker and sicker.
You lied through your lips: "It was only one beer..."
How many untruths did you want her to hear?
Sobriety vanished— and addiction drew near.
It was wearing the face of the devil you feared.
You slept with the bottle, your wife disappeared.
Now your nights feel possessed by the sins you revered.
Ain't no moonlight when she's gone.

Beat down. Broke down. Still, you got up.
Trying to escape—you found love in that cup.
But that's not love in that cup—that's poison you swallow,
And death takes a bow, when you kiss on that bottle.
Wolf under the moon; solitude is your friend.
Conversations with self—the voice from within.
It's your angel in this fight. It's your Muhammad Ali.
But will you choose long life...or Long Island iced tea?
And that just might be the final decision you make.
I've seen many folks fade into an alcoholic's wake—
Seen the cold repossession of luxurious cars,
Wedding rings get pawned, and drunks locked behind bars.
I've seen the wealthy go broke, and the healthy fall ill,
Having the time of your life—until alcohol kills.

A battle is brewing. Conflicted within.
Recovery is calling, but so is the gin.
Your focus is fixed on refusing to drink,
Pouring that demon juice down in the sink.
Smashing the bottle and breaking the glass,
Striving for sobriety—hoping it lasts.
Nausea, sweating, anxiety, nerves...
Craving a sip, but you're fighting the urge.

Missing your lady—her smile was your light.
True love for your Luna, your guide in the night.
Moon Woman. Goddess. The guard of your heart,
Choose love in the light over drinks in the dark.
'Cause ain't no moonlight when she's gone.

THE HEALER WORE HEELS

Mama say, "Son, don't you break no hearts."
Daddy say, "Be heartless—keep these women in the dark."
Mama say, "Son, treat your woman like a queen."
Daddy say, "These women only good for certain things."
Mama say, "Son, sometimes silence is the choice."
Daddy say, "Speak up, and let the nation hear your voice."
Mama say, "Son, when you step, move with caution."
Daddy say, "Stomp, and shake the ground when you're walkin'."

Mama say, "A car is just a way to get around."
Daddy say, "A Benz will give you status in this town."
Mama say, "Your friends should all be welcomed to your house."
Daddy say, "Those bastards bet not show up unannounced."
Mama say, "Make money, just don't let it take your peace."
Daddy say, "Get paid, 'cause you can rest when you're deceased."
Mama say, "Get married—find a woman on your level."
Daddy say, "Stay single—all these women turn to devils."

Mama say, "You better tell your daddy watch his mouth."
Daddy say, "I stand on every word that just came out."
Mama say, "If women turn to devils, so do men."
Daddy say, "Well Eve's the one who walked us into sin."
Mama say, "But Adam was a fool to even listen."
Daddy say, "That's why a woman's place is in the kitchen."
Mama say, "Don't say that—chauvinism isn't fun."
Daddy say, "Be quiet, girl, I'm talking to my son."

Daddy say, "A woman should be barefoot in a dress."
Daddy say, "A working woman's paycheck should be less."
Daddy say, "A woman should look down when she is walking."
Daddy say, "A woman should shut up when men are talking."
Daddy say, "A woman isn't smart enough to manage."
Daddy say, "A woman should be making him a sandwich."
Daddy say, "A woman's too emotional to lead."
Daddy say, "A woman cannot focus when she bleeds."
Daddy say, "A woman should stay in her residence."
Daddy say, "A woman never will be President."

Daddy grabbed his chest and started screaming for his woman.
9-1-1 was called—the operator... was a woman.
The ambulance arrived—the EMT... it was a woman.
Speeding through the traffic—and the driver... was a woman.
Hospital admittance—and the nurse... it was a woman.
Surgery performed—guess who the doctor was... a woman.
Daddy damn near died—who saved his life... it was a woman.
So now when Daddy prays, he knows he's praying...
to a woman.

UNCLE CHARLIE: WOKE AT HIS OWN FUNERAL

Uncle Charlie woke up at his funeral service.
The pastor passed out, and the people were looking nervous.
See, everyone had gathered to put old Charlie to rest,
But Uncle Charlie had a few things to get off of his chest.

And it started with the dress that his widow was wearing—
Too tight and too short, and the people were staring.
So while his widow was sitting there trying to look cute,
Uncle Charlie was dead in an ugly ass suit.

Wrinkled in the front, old shirt with missing buttons,
Pants were too tight—no shoes, socks, or nothing.
Tie didn't match. Fedora hat had a hole.
Old chain around his neck, made of imitation gold.

No, Charlie wasn't feeling his funeral fashion—
In his mind, the angels in heaven would be laughing.

So before the obituary was able to be read,
Uncle Charlie sat up in his casket and said:

As the person who's here to be memorialized,
I'd like to call out my wife for all of your lies.
Yeah, you only arrived to be part of the show—
No respect for my life, but you'll reap what you sow.
I have thousand-dollar suits in my closet right now,
So why lay me to rest in this poverty style?

It's almost as if you are saving my suits
For your new man to wear on his dates out with you.
And speaking of dates, I've been dead for three weeks,
And not once has a tear ever rolled down your cheek.

Not once did you cry. You don't care that I died,
'Cause I'm simply worth more to you dead than alive.
Oh, I know about the secret insurance you took out,
And my money you stashed in your sister's account.

I guess business is business—ain't that what they say?
But who would have thought you would do me this way.
If I could, I would cry, but I'll laugh in the end—
'Cause I won't rest in peace 'til I have my revenge.

And Fred, my best friend... you been chasing my spouse,
'Cause my soul saw you creep out the back of my house.
And since I'm deceased, it's not technically cheating,
But I will haunt your ass until your heart stops beating!

I will spook you every night for as long as you live—
I will turn into a ghost and scare the hell out your kids!
Now take off my clothes, my watch, and my rings.
Can't you wait till I'm buried before wearing my things?

And why are my car keys even in your possession?
Are you driving my Mercedes? It's time for a confession...
Have you and my widow ever shared the same bed?
Have you ever slept together, even before I was dead?

Tell the truth and shame the devil—I'm daring you, Fred,
'Cause if I find out you crossed me, they'll be burying you, Fred.
Oh, now you're afraid? Should I call you scary, Fred?
You know there's room for another body in this cemetery, Fred.
There's room for two bodies in this cemetery, Fred.
They're looking for new bodies... for this cemetery, Fred.

And just when Uncle Charlie was about to go hard,
The pastor woke up and said, "Praise to the Lord!
We have gathered here today on this sorrowful occasion
To put Charlie to rest—yes, his life was amazing.

And the scriptures will tell us God controls the situation—
Somebody pass around the plate, I need to collect my donations.
In the beginning, the Most High said, 'Let there be light...'
But if I don't pay these bills, the church will not have any lights."

And at that point, Charlie had enough of all the madness—
People laughing in the back, there was hardly any sadness.
He wondered if anyone ever cared about his life:
Pastor wanted money, his best friend wanted his wife.

No flowers from his job. A lot of family didn't come.
There was no love being shown for all the good he had done.
So he flashed the middle finger and he closed the casket tight,
Took his last breath, and asked God to bring his soul to the light.

Rest in Paradise, Uncle Charlie.

SCORPIO VOICE

Let me be blunt—Uncle Charlie got played.
And I saw it coming three stares, two fake tears, and one awkward eulogy ago.

Scorpio rule #1:
If your best friend's always around your woman,
He either wants your life, your wife, or both.

Charlie missed it—because he saw love.
I see patterns.
I see posture.
I see silence that speaks louder than loyalty ever could.

People like me get called suspicious.
But paranoia is just pattern recognition in a world full of snakes.
So no—I don't trust easy.
And I don't miss signs.
Cause once you've been backstabbed enough,
you start measuring people by the sharpness of their smiles.

That's why I stay two steps ahead.
That's why my daughters won't get blindsided—
Not on my watch.
Not while I'm breathing.
I read the room, the subtext, the secret agendas.

And if protecting my princesses makes me overbearing?

Good.

I'd rather be their storm shelter than their obituary writer.

DADDY'S BABY GIRL

(My Angel Then, My Angel Now)

Daddy's baby girl.
Daddy's very precious baby girl.
All grown up, but still my pearl,
And you remain the axis upon which forever spins my entire world.

I am wowed by the memories of you as a child—
In fact, my mind constantly rewinds
The mental movies of you,
And the things you used to do
To make me laugh and make me smile.

You were then what you are now—
The vital valve to that miracle muscle that pumps in my chest.
Yes... you are Daddy's heart.
And that's why the sadness I see in your eyes right now
Is completely tearing your daddy apart.

No—don't turn away.
Please, look me in my face
And tell me everything with you is all right.
And if it's not all right,
Tell Daddy what's wrong
And I promise you—a change gonna come tonight.

Now... was it an argument or a fight?
A discussion or disagreement?
Did he call you out of your name?
And is he really the one you want to be with?

Did he get mad and raise his voice?
Worse than that... did he raise his hand?
The silent treatment will not solve this issue—
And don't you lie to me to protect that man.

You are Daddy's baby girl.
Daddy's very precious baby girl.
All grown up, but still my pearl.
And you remain the light of the moon—
Forever illuminating your daddy's world.

Remember that Cinderella dress
And the way you'd do that cute little twirl?
Those tiny white patent leather shoes...
The bobby socks...
And the way you'd shake that beautiful head full of curls.

My angel then, my angel now—
I'd sacrifice life to permanently remove your frown.
You see, these men... they come and go.
But it's your Daddy—and your God—
Who will always be around.

Tell me now... what happened to you
Before I walked into your residence?
Was his declaration of love for you
Delivered with the slightest bit of hesitance?

Did he forget whose daughter you were?
Did he forget your maiden name?
Did he forget that your father would come for him
With the force of a ferocious hurricane?

See, my aim is not to interfere—
I trust your judgment, I truly do.
But it's hard for me to stand by and watch
When I know that something is bothering you.

You are Daddy's baby girl.
Daddy's very precious baby girl.
All grown up, but still my pearl.
And you remain the jasmine flower
Forever blooming in your daddy's world.

Born as a princess, matured into a queen,
Grew up to be one of the most magnificent
Human beings my eyes have ever seen.

Someone would say I'm biased
And my point of view is not objective.
But I stand by what I say—
And I don't apologize for being overprotective.

You're a diamond... a pearl...
And should always be treated as such.
So if any man should harm you—
It's ashes to ashes, and dust to dust.

What do you mean I have it twisted?
What do you mean I have it wrong?
What do you mean he makes you joyful
And you love your happy home?

What do you mean he reads you scriptures?
What do you mean he prays with you?
What do you mean that he has promised,
In the name of God,
To spend all of his days with you?

What do you mean... that you are pregnant?
What do you mean... you're having a son?

Well... I guess... I should be... happy.
And I should... put away my gun?

Congratulations, baby girl.
I always knew God would send you the right guy.

SCORPIO VOICE – FREEDOM WAS THE FINAL STING

Well, well... you made it this far.
I'll admit—I didn't think you would.
You survived the sting of passion,
the weight of sorrow,
the mirror of your own reflection...
and didn't fold.

But now comes the reckoning.

This is where illusions burn.
Where silence breaks.
Where the fight for freedom stops sounding poetic
and starts hitting personal.

I've walked through fire for less.
I've bled for names most people can't even say out loud.
That's the Scorpio way.
In these pages, you'll face injustice raw and unfiltered—
not just in the streets,
but in the home,
in the mirror,
in your God.

This is liberation.
Not granted, but taken.
Not clean, but necessary.

So take my hand—
but don't expect comfort.
We don't come to be saved.
We come to be scorched...
and survive it.

Now turn the page...
*and enter **The Final Sting**.*

FREEDOM WAS THE FINAL STING

(LIBERATION)

PARANOID FETUS

(Born Into the Fire)

Paranoid fetus.
Unborn child scared to live—
Help me, Black Jesus.

Paranoid fetus.
Afraid to leave the womb—
This world don't want me here,
Black Jesus.

From inside my mother's stomach,
I can feel the blade of hatred.
Buzzards circle before my birth—
Because I'm Black…
Have I been snake-bit?

The angels call: "Come to the light."
But I'm not convinced this world's sacred.
I've seen too many Black babies
Blessed with breath—
Only for death to come and take it.

Mother's breathing
Is steady increasing.
The birth of me is not far away.
But if given the choice, I'd stay inside—
What worth is life
In the end of days?

So to God, I pray:

Heavenly Father...
Let not the levies of my mother's birth canal be cracked.
Let not her water break,
Nor her contractions intensify,
Coming painfully back to back.

For my wish is to remain where I am at—
Attached to the placenta,
Surrounded by the fluids that comfort me
Within the amniotic sac.

And mother...
Where is my father at?
Does he know how close you are?
Has he proceeded to grab
The already prepared hospital bag
And placed it on the backseat of the car?

The journey is not far,
But we're traveling fast.
Mother is feeling quite nauseous;
Daddy's stepping hard upon the gas.

I say—Whoa, Daddy.
Don't you run that red light.
I know I've got to come,
But I don't want to come tonight.

Besides—what's the rush,
When we're in the last days?
This world's full of suicide,
Homicide, rape...

This world is full of genocide,
Apartheid, and hate.
This world is full of stereotypes,
Parasites, and snakes.

That's why I am a paranoid fetus.
Unborn child scared to live—
Help me, Black Jesus.

I am a paranoid fetus.
Afraid to leave the womb—
This world don't want me here,
Black Jesus.

From inside my mother's stomach,
I can feel outside aggression.
Maggots cry for my demise.
If I'm born alive...
Will I suffer depression?

The angels call: "Come to the light."
But I'm not convinced this world will love me.
Seen too many Black brothers jailed this year—
I don't want no cop to cuff me.

Seen too many Black bodies drop this year—
I don't trust nobody but me.
Seen so many Black babies hurt this year—
I just want my God to hug me.

Cervix dilated.
Eight centimeters wide.
I fight against the birth
As I feel myself slide.

Doctor, stand back—
With your mask and your gloves on.
Don't deliver me
Until the guns and the drugs are gone.

My life is not a love song.
My people sing the blues.
Another brother murdered—
See the footage on the news.

Priests abusing children.
Child molested—someone's son.
That's why I've been feeling nervous
Since trimester number one.

Mama, I don't want to come.
Please don't push me out tonight.
I know you and Dad will love me...
But this world ain't spinning right.

Terrorism.
Deep racism.
Anti-intellectualism.
Separatism.
Phony religion.
Intolerance of individualism.

I've made my decision.
I don't wanna be born.
Mama, stop pushing—
I don't wanna be born.

Doctor, stop pulling—
I don't wanna be born.
And Daddy...
Please stop smiling—

I don't wanna be born.

Too late.
I've already been born.
I'm breathing on my own—
I've already been born.

Umbilical cord cut—
I've already been born.
Lying on my mother's chest—
I've already been born.

Young, gifted, and Black—
I've already been born.
And since it was God who insisted I be born...

Perhaps this Scorpio
Was born to spit spoken word poetry
Strong enough
To change this crazy world.

WHY NOT NOW?
(A Generational Call to Action)

Why now, you ask?
And I respond with fire in my chest—why not now?
If now is the new "back then,"
Then why not rise like they rose back then, when
Revolution wasn't an outfit—
It was a diet. A prayer. A weapon. A sin.

Why now, you ask again?
And again, I reply with flames in my chest: Why not now?
If not now, then when—where—and how
Will we answer the question posed by the heartbroken child,
Eyes wide, voice trembling:
"Why did your generation let our generation drown?"

If your elders were like mine,
You've heard the phrase, "Don't put off for tomorrow
What you have the power to change today."
So I say:
Rise up, my people—there's a war against our kind.
And my choice of artillery is an educated mind.
'Cause we're outmanned and outgunned—no match for military combat.
But the power in our brain—that's where the real nuclear bomb is at.
So let's all stay in contact, take my phone number down.
I know a sister named Harriet with a railroad underground.
I know a doctor named King pushin' peaceful resistance,
Believing we shall overcome through prayer and persistence.
I know a brother named Malcolm with a different type vibe—
Gun in hand, he's at that window and he's peeking outside.
Three different approaches and three different styles...

But still the same goal: equality right now!
Justice right now!
Liberty right now!
And still... you have the nerve to keep asking me why now?
"Why not now" will forever be my answer.
Let not the disease of procrastination be the new Black cancer.

Why not now—after the Zimmerman jury?
Why not now—after Ferguson, Missouri?
Why not now—after Cleveland, Ohio...
The church in South Carolina where evil sat beside us,
Smiled during prayer,
And slaughtered the choir?

Why not now,
When we are all still surviving—
Still breathing,
Still grieving,
Still being hunted
In a system that was never designed for us to win?

Warriors, remember who you are.
Your rage is righteous. Your silence is sin.
And if we don't fight back with brilliance,
We will be buried in the shadows of what could have been.

So I ask, again...
Why not now?

SCORPIO VOICE

They always say,
"Be patient. Be peaceful. Be still."
But if Harriet had waited...
there'd be no tracks in the soil,
no lanterns in the night,
no footsteps toward freedom.

If Frederick had waited...
they'd still be reading chains instead of chapters.

If a Scorpio waited to grow wings,
he'd be a flying lobster.
Ugly, confused, and crawling in circles.
But we were born for evolution—
to sting, to break, to rise.

And I'm tired of the sermons
preaching slow progress
to people bleeding out in real time.
Justice delayed is a setup.
Revolution postponed is a casket waiting.

We don't need rage without reason.
We need fire with direction.
Mind sharp as our wounds.
Moves made with purpose.

No more waiting.
No more asking.
No more shame in where we started.

Now flip the lights on...
and see what brilliance the ghetto birthed.
Watch how survival became an art.
And how we—
we became the masterpiece..

EVERYTHING THE GHETTO IS

(And I... Am Amazing)

I am everything the ghetto is.
I am the concrete cracked and torn apart.
The sidewalk broken like young Black hearts.
The cement damaged for years and years,
The graveled surface that catches the tears
Of children who walk to school in fear
As bullets buzz right by their ears.
I am everything the ghetto is.

I am graffiti painted upon the walls.
Books replaced with basketballs.
Pitbull barks disturbing the peace,
The darker skin you have the nerve to bleach,
The tattooed arms you cover with sleeves,
And the kinky hair you hide with weaves.
I am everything the ghetto is.

I am the taco truck on every block,
The liquor store, the gambling spot.
The motel room where lovers creep,
The fiends who smoke while others sleep.
The alleyway where drugs are bought,
The public schools where nothing's taught,
Murdered men whose dreams are over,
The next of kin who scream Jehovah,
The child too young to witness death—
Age five when I saw that man's last breath.

And yes...
I am everything the ghetto is and more.
Much more.
So much more that your labels will not name me,
Your devils will not claim me,
Your chains bring pain, but I refuse to let them contain or restrain me.
The blood of African royalty runs through my veins...
And that's the DNA that sustains me.

I am everything the ghetto is and more.
I am the voice of the lion, majestic roar.
And if Black Lives Matter—who's keeping the score?
I am the floor that caught Malcolm's falling flesh,
The balcony backdrop of Martin Luther's death,
The river bottom that held Emmett Till,
The Birmingham church where four angels were killed.
I am the fist of resistance lifted up to the stars,
The face of the mahogany movement here to claim what is ours.
Yes, I am everything the ghetto is.
And I...
Am amazing.

SCORPIO VOICE

The hood don't own you.
It raised you, maybe.
Tried to break you, definitely.
But it damn sure doesn't get to define you.

You don't have to inherit your zip code's fate.
And you sure as hell don't have to wear someone else's limitations like
hand-me-downs.
It ain't about where you're at...
It's about where you're going.

SCENE:
Park Bench Outside an Abandoned School – Morning – 10:28 am

Elder leans back, cigar in hand, eyes scanning the crumbling bricks.

"They shut it down. Said the test scores were too low.
Told us we were unteachable. Disposable."

He looks at the young man sitting beside him—hoodie, notebook,
hungry eyes.

"I wrote my first book on this same bench.
Didn't wait for a system to see me.
Didn't wait for a hero to save me.
You don't wait either."

The young man nods slowly.

"Be your own damn miracle," the elder says, rising.

QUEEN DOWN
(The Killing of Sonya Massey)

Sonya, don't go to that stove, near that water.
That killer don't care that you're somebody's daughter.
That killer don't care you're a parent of two—
There's death in his eyes, and he's staring at you.

He told you to turn off the pot, but don't listen.
You'll probably be shot by that cop in your kitchen.
I know it's your home, and your home is your palace—
But he harbors hate, and his heart's full of malice.

His actions are callous—he'll kill you for fun.
When you call for assistance, the savages come.
That man means murder. He's Lucifer's son.
Now who gave that devil a badge and a gun?

Who gave that devil a badge and a gun?
She knew... he was a devil with a badge and a gun.
So she rebuked that devil with a badge and a gun:

"I rebuke you in the name of Jesus..."
"You better f**king not. I swear to God, I will shoot you right in your
f**king face!"
"I'm sorry..."
BANG! BANG! BANG!

Queen down. Queen down. How can he ignore?
There's blood mixed with water all over the floor.
Two minutes at least, no assistance is rendered—
He wants her deceased. That's his evil agenda.

And there she lies... her face to the sky.
He may have killed her body, but her soul still flies.
Spirit don't die. Keep her memory alive—
'Cause it wasn't the boiling water that caused her death in July.

Murdered in 2024... can't take too much more.
Whether you believe it or not, our people are at war.

So it's time we wake up and realize
Who and what it is we are fighting for...

Be well as you dwell with the ancestors...
Sonya Massey.

SCORPIO VOICE

She didn't die over a pot of water.

She died because this country doesn't see Black women as human.
She died because a badge became a license.
Because rage got more grace than her Black skin did.
Because her cry for help got misread as a threat.

Queen Down.

And you want me to believe in freedom?

I've seen too many queens fall. Too many mothers mourn.
Too many names turned hashtags while murderers keep their pensions.
And I'm tired of speeches, tired of candlelight vigils,
tired of patience being our only path forward.

Scorpios don't do delusion.
We don't wait for justice to wake up—we drag it out of hiding.

They call it freedom.
But I call it what it is—
an illusion.

Now move to the next page, and let's stop pretending.

FREEDOM IS AN ILLUSION
(The Truth Behind the Mask)

I woke up,
Feelin' froggy, y'all—
So I decided to leap.

I jumped to the conclusion
That freedom...
Is an illusion.
And we, as Black folk,
Ain't never gonna feel safe out on these streets.

We're in The Matrix—
And that rabbit hole is deep.
And the more we dig,
The more we discover...

That sisters and brothers
Need to do more
Than just protest, pray, and preach.

'Cause while we're down on our knees,
Askin' the Lord to protect our souls—
The enemy is above us
At point-blank range,
Ready to pump our bodies full of bullet holes.

It's out of control.
And it's been that way for weeks,
Months,
Years,
Decades,
Centuries.

Ever since the slave ship hit the Motherland,
And the other man put the brother man in chains.
Drug us into captivity
And made us build this nation over here.

And let me be clear—
For some of our struggles,
We bear responsibility too.

What fool allows the hooded hater to hit him,
And instead of hitting the hooded hater back,
He hauls off—
And knocks the hell out of you.

Same thing with gang-banging:
Some bang red,
And some bang blue...

But the Ku Klux Klan
Don't give a damn
What gang you hang with or bang with—
The only thing they're claiming is hatred,
And the one they want to see hanging...
Is you.

And it's such a sad sight
To see such beautiful Black bodies
Swingin' from the trees.
We're yelling we shall overcome
When we need to be screaming:
Eradicate the hate
Before hate has the opportunity
To eradicate we.

Much love and respect
For Dr. King and the legacy he produced—
But I can't turn the other cheek...
Not while my neck is hangin' in a noose.

Now, who got the juice?
Me.
And I'm willin' to pass you a glass.

They're servin' pork chops and pig feet,
But as your brother,
I'm gonna ask you to fast.

'Cause I see through the mask—
And I recognize the evil eyes
That's hiding inside of it.

Get away from me, Satan.
I ain't buyin' what you're sellin',
'Cause I've already been sold
On the blessings the Good Lord has provided.

Good and evil have collided
In a world that's sinking into quicksand.
Everybody wants to be a starter,
But somebody has to be the sixth man.

Sit back,
Watch and wait—
Strategize and calculate.
Anticipate the attack...
Then counterattack
And eliminate the hate.

The struggle is real.
And there's really no debate.
Many may sympathize—
But how many can really relate?

'Cause they ain't never walked in a Black man's shoes.
Never been kidnapped,
Beaten and abused.
Never been snatched from their land and enslaved.
Never built a nation—
And didn't get paid.

Never been hunted by the Ku Klux Klan.
Never been considered three-fifths of a man.
Never been a Black woman whose son was shot dead.
Never been raped on a plantation bed.
Never been a nanny who was treated real rotten,
Raisin' other people's kids
While your own kids are out pickin' cotton.
Never been profiled inside of a store.
Never been called the N-word
And sent off to war.

What I'm sayin' is—
They ain't never been Black.
And if they've never been Black,
How the hell can they tell Black folks how to act?

We go to sleep havin' dreams
And wake up after nightmares—
Thrown in a ring
With a demon
Who don't fight fair.

But keep kickin', my sisters.
And keep punchin', my brothers.
Cause if we ain't got nothin' else...

I pray to God
That we always have
Each other.

I'M TIRED
(A Funeral We Keep Repeating)

I'm tired of dressing up
From head to toe in black.
Casket's opened up—
My friend is on his back.
I hear his mother cry.
I see his children weep.
They ask me how he died—
Killed by the police.

And so I pray...
Father, your son said, **"Please forgive them, for they know not what
they do."**
And far be it from me to be the one to question You.
But God, I just can't help it.
My soul is so unnerved.
My spirit's feeling weary,
And my conscience is disturbed.

Those cops—they are your children.
You've fathered them all too.
So should not they be punished
For the evil that they do?

I was raised to hide my cries,
Disguise my fears—be prepared to fight.
But if these tears escape my eyes,
You will witness rain for many nights.

When I say that I can't breathe,
That don't mean to choke me dead.
And when I raise up both my hands,
That doesn't mean aim for my head.

Trigger-happy, so full of hate,
They show no love for young Black men.
You thought that curb was painted red?
No—those are bloodstains from my friends.

When will it end, God? When will it end?
You know, it seems like the 1960s again.

We move forward and get pushed back,
And people say progression is what we lack.
Police use aggression 'cause our color is Black,
Arrested for possession—cops are planting the crack.
Behind bars, stressing—this depression is whack.
And where's our protection when we're under attack?

When will it end, God? When will it end?
You know, it seems like the 1960s again.

And I'm tired of dressing up
From head to toe in black.
Casket's opened up—
My friend is on his back.
I hear his mother cry.
I see his children weep.
Asked me how he died...

And I shouldn't have to say—
He was killed by the police.

SCORPIO VOICE

It starts young.

Pretty brown girls, smart and fierce,
seduced by menthol kisses
and ads dressed up like magazine covers.

They're selling smoke to our daughters now.
Bubblegum blunts. Candy-coated cancer.
Wrapped in pink and pain.
Same poison—just prettier packaging.

They want them hooked early—
but me? I lost everything late.

I'll never forget sitting beside my mother's bed,
holding her hand through plastic tubes,
counting breaths like borrowed time.

I still hear the hiss of her oxygen tank.
Still see the outline of her breath
fighting to stay inside her.

Death ain't always loud.
Sometimes it's slow,
silent,
corporate.

SCENE:
Schoolyard - Morning - 11:19 am

A teenage girl giggles behind the bleachers.
Cherry vape in hand,
Smiling while snapping smoke-filled selfies.
She doesn't know—
It's a funeral dress rehearsal.

A cherry-wood casket is waiting for her.

LUNGS
(From Personal Loss to Collective Survival)

MY MOTHER'S LUNGS
(Personal Grief)

Recovery's not easy—
Leave that cigarette in the pack.
COPD, diabetes, emphysema, heart attack.
Calculate adjusted lifespan—
Level down the more you smoke…
Chop ten years off your existence,
Live in fear of deadly strokes.

I'm no expert on tobacco,
But I know more than I'd like—
'Cause I watched my mother suffer.
I was by her bed each night.

Breathing treatment. Breathing tank.
Oxygen machine at home…
Plastic tube inside her nose…
Her lung capacity was gone.

Oximeter for her finger—
This device, I knew it well.
Used to monitor and measure
Oxygen in red blood cells.

Mama, focus on your breathing.
Don't be nervous, I'll be near.
Hold my hand, I'll never leave you…
Doctor, hurry up in here!

Something is heavy on her chest plate—
Putting pressure on her rib cage.
Her lungs are locked in battle.
She's barely breathing—
I'm yelling, "Death, Wait!"

But it was too late...
I watched her health deteriorate.
The tobacco industry continues
To escalate the Black mortality rate.

She hadn't smoked in over a decade—
But the damage was already done.
The cigarette cartel succeeded...
In making me a motherless son.

And sadly...
Tobacco's attack is not yet done.

Smoke hurt my mother's lungs
Porum Pom-Pom-Pom
She passed in '21
Porum Pom-Pom-Pom
Her passing left me numb
Porum Pom-Pom-Pom
Rum Pom-Pom-Pom...
Rum Pom-Pom-Pom...

MY PEOPLE'S LUNGS
(Public Fight)

"Hands up, don't shoot"—
They say from the North to the South.
An hour later, your hands go up…
Putting that cigarette inside your mouth.

The secondhand smoke
Floats through your dwelling's ventilation—
Exposing others to diseases
Caused by passive inhalation.

Ignorance is no excuse.
But being targeted is a thing.
Big Tobacco's locked and loaded—
Replacing bullets with nicotine.

Our communities in the crosshairs—
Direct line of fire.
And since we know that Black Lives Matter,
Drop those cigarettes and that lighter.

While we fight for social justice,
Reparations, and equal income…
The industry of tobacco
Attacks our respiratory system.

Pay attention to what they're doing.
Their devious tactics should alarm us.
Buying billboards and bus benches,
Promoting products that will harm us.

Aiming for our children—
Got them vaping in the schools.

Creating flavors to entice them...
There's a war against our youth.

We have to be more careful—
Call it conscious, call it woke.
If not, we'll lose our future
As it all goes up in smoke.

We can see our people dying.
Lungs attacked around the clock.
If it's not inside your home,
Tobacco's surely on your block.

Church, liquor store, motel...
Church, liquor store, motel...

I pray that the cigarettes
You bought from the store
Don't leave you choking
In a cheap motel.

Because tobacco...
Is coming for us.

Smoke hurt my people's lungs
Porum Pom-Pom-Pom
They're passing one by one
Porum Pom-Pom-Pom
These passings left me numb
Porum Pom-Pom-Pom
Rum Pom-Pom-Pom...
Rum Pom-Pom-Pom...

SCORPIO VOICE

They call us intense.
But I call it tuned in.

See, you can't just hear what your woman says—you have to hear what she
doesn't say...
The silence. The sigh. The weight she carries while you're out marching.
You're forgetting the mission starts where you lay your head at night.

You wanna save the world?
Start by saving her.

Brother, you better figure out what a Scorpio already knows—
The real revolution is the one that rescues your relationship.

SCENE:
Living Room - Late Night - 11:07 pm

His queen's asleep on the couch. Hair wrapped.
Arms crossed like a final verdict.

Half-finished homework sheet on the coffee table.
Backpacks tossed in the corner.
Cold smothered chicken still sitting on the stove.

He walks in—
smelling like protest, voice hoarse from yelling.
Steps over her shoes but doesn't even kiss her cheek.

"You win the revolution yet?" she asks, eyes still closed.

He doesn't answer.

She already knows.
And in that silence... something starts to die.

REVOLUTION IN THE HOME
(The Fight Starts at the Front Door)

So you want to be an activist
And wear your dashiki,
Blow out your Afro
And protest on a weekly.

Wear black leather coats
And black leather pants,
Trying to bring back the 60s
In that Black Power stance.

But would you step to the forefront
When the front line of your family needs to be manned?
Would you raise that Black fist
And show that wedding ring on your hand?

When your queen needs her king—
Would you stand right beside her?
Quit complaining about the heat, Negro—
She needs you to walk through that fire.

There needs to be a revolution...
In the home.

So don't talk about it—be about it.
Save that Black woman.
She's the backbone of your family,
You've got to praise that Black woman.

But you want to be heard,
So you're yelling Revolution!
Screaming Black Lives Matter
And demanding restitution.

No argument from me,
'Cause see—I'm feeling that fight.
But do not neglect that woman at home
With your children at night.

Homework help, dinner and a snack,
Bathe and tuck 'em in... they ask:
"Where is Daddy at?"

She's covering your tracks,
Telling them that you're at work.
Retreats to her bedroom,
Where she cries because it hurts.

Why?
Because it hurts.
Man, you can't even call?

She don't know if you're in jail—
Or in someone else's drawers.

She's all about the cause,
Visualizing the bigger picture.
Holding down the Homefront,
And wishing she was out there fighting with ya.

But night after night,
All alone, she must sleep.
The government ain't been overthrown—
And your ass ain't been home in weeks.

There needs to be a revolution...
In the home.

But I get it.

You want to be an activist
And wear your dashiki,
Blow out your Afro
And protest on a weekly.

Wear black leather coats,
And black leather pants,
Trying to bring back the 60s
In that Black Power stance.

But how militant would you get
If you need to make sure your family is fine?

Would you put the movement on pause—
And dedicate yourself
To spending a little bit of quality family time?

Would you read to your son?
Sing a song to your daughter?
Give your lady a hug,
And keep your love life in order?

And what I mean is:
Making your queen scream
Until the clouds open up
And start pouring down champagne and rainwater.

The foundation of our fight
Is rooted in the relationships we have with one another.

I'm talking:
Father to mother.
Sister to brother.
Friend to friend...
And lover to lover.

So listen, my brother—
Please make sure your relationship with your woman is in tune.

After all,
We want her to bandage our cuts and bruises,
And never pour seasoning salt
Inside of our open war wounds.

Four hundred years,
And we've paid a very heavy cost.

But what good is winning the battle on the outside
When your family becomes the casualty—
And the war on the inside...
Is ultimately lost?

There needs to be a revolution...
In the home.

MONOPOLY
(When the Board is the Battlefield)

Imagine being born into a world that resembles a game of Monopoly—
A world where Blacks can roll the dice, but can never purchase property.
Commanded never to pass Go, and if you do, cops say, "Damn you!"
Did you NOT see that invisible stop sign that you just ran through?

Now take your Black ass to jail, and you will not be just visitin'.
Spend **$50** to bail out, and return to the poverty you've been living in.
Bad luck with the dice, no matter how you might roll it—
You cannot buy a railroad, but you can be railroaded.

Pay the luxury tax—that's **$100**.
Pay the income tax—that's **$200**.
Land on other people's property—have to give them your dollars.
Every time you make a move, seems like you're spending more dollars.

And the banker is no better, because he's laughing in your face.
You don't qualify for a loan—we don't lend cash to your race.
We only lend to certain people, and that certainly isn't you.
They say we all are treated equal... and that certainly isn't true.

But to give you a little hope, there's a square that says Chance.
Land on that and pick a card—perhaps we'll allow you to advance.
But more likely than not, you'll have to forfeit more money.
Pay the bank **$100**, based on the card you picked up, dummy.

Or maybe it's the card that you just happened to be handed—
Community Chest, advance three spaces...
now look where you just landed:
Boardwalk with hotels. Can you afford to pay the rent?
I think not, because you're broke and probably living in a tent.

A corner space on the board says **Free Parking** over there.

If you're considering prostitution, you can start it over there.
Another option? Be a dealer. Sell some drugs to kill your kind.
There's no funding for your schools, so be a student of committing crime.

Try your hand at Gangster rap—better yet, just join a gang.
Maybe start a YouTube channel, that could be your claim to fame.
Play some basketball—maybe you can make it to the league.
Real life Monopoly was never made for black folks to succeed.

Now this game I used to love is a reminder of despair.
So when I see it, I don't smile—I want to toss it in the air.
Break the board and burn the pieces, something new is on the way.
Redistribution of the wealth—we'll make new rules before we play.

We'll rebuild from what was broken—make it better than before.
Right is right and fair is fair—we won't be begging anymore.
Our board is rooted in black culture, there's creation in our veins.
They can play Monopoly—we'll play the Liberation game.

SCORPIO VOICE

You know what I hate more than the lie?
That we hand our children loaded dice
And tell them to smile while they lose.

But Scorpio don't do blind obedience.
We question, we challenge, we rewrite.

I'm done pretending this game was ever fair.
Done watching us play with broken pieces.

Our youth need to know the truth.

SCENE:
Kitchen Table - Summer Morning - 11:21 am

A child throws her Monopoly money in the air.

"Why we always lose, Daddy?"

He looks at the board... then at her.

"Because it wasn't made for us to win, baby girl.
But watch this..."

He grabs a sharpie.
Renames Boardwalk to Malcolm X Way.
Puts Harriet Tubman on the $500 bill.
Rewrites the rules with her watching.

"This ain't their game no more.
This is ours."

THE CUB BECOMES KING

(Son of a Revolutionary)

When you thought of your father, it was Daddy stop teasing.

When I thought of my father, it was, I hope he still breathing.

I prayed for his safety, prayed he was still living—

Grade school nightmares of my father in state prison.

I listened to the whispers, heard what the government said.

Mass incarceration, that machine must be fed.

Dead was my family structure, there was a war against our kind.

Why was 50% of the prison population looking like relatives of mine?

Never mind—'cause I never signed up to see my father in that hellhole.

Hard time living, life in prison—the design of COINTELPRO.

No relationship with Daddy. Sadly, so much damage was done.

Thus was the life of a revolutionary's son.

Thus was the life of an inmate's son.

When you thought of your father, it was fun, Daddy fun.

When I thought of my father, it was run, Daddy run.

Escape from San Quentin. Flee the U.S. of A.

If God's good, he'll change the world—and we'll be together one day.

Or maybe we won't. Perhaps this is the end.

I'm age eight, contemplating never seeing my father again.

My little brother is six, I wrap my arm around him calmly:

Stop crying, Shambulia—we have to take care of Mommy.

We are true Zulu Warriors. Young lions, remember?

We have to be brave like Daddy and don't ever surrender.

So what if he's gone and can't watch us grow up?

When we graduate, we know he can't show up.

And when we need advice—we know he can't provide it.

I wanted to cry too—but I learned how to hide it.

Besides, I'm the oldest. Just follow my lead.

I'll wipe away your tears and catch every drop of blood that you bleed.

Indeed, I was afraid—but played the role of the bravest one.

Thus was the life of a revolutionary's son.

Thus was the life of an inmate's son.

When you thought of your father, it was surfboards and smiles.

When I thought of my father, it was parole board denials.

No burgers and barbecues—just murder charges and falsely accused.

Prison escapee with nothing to lose—

America's most wanted on the evening news.

When you thought of your parents, it was husband and wife.

When I thought of my parents:

Mother raised me—Daddy lived the fugitive life.

I saw the rise in private prisons—was that pipeline meant for me?

Young target of the system—I've been woke since the age of three.

Saw my community come undone, fall apart, and lose its way.

A childhood interrupted—Black boy had no time to play.

When I thought about my father, my feelings felt like rain.

So to be who I've become, I had to go through all that pain.

And thus was the life of a revolutionary's son.

This is the fight... and never will I run.

POETICALLY POSSESSED
(A Poet's Protest)

I am a poet—
Poetically possessed by the spirit of Amiri Baraka,
Generational general, Zulu Shaka.
Strong like minerals—Boom Shakalaka.
Chain-breaking miracle—Hakuna Matata.

Walk down, stomp down.
Who's the imposter?
Spook who sat by the door—
Wearing locs, eating lobster.

Revolution... revolve.
Revolution... revolve.
Identify the problem, seek a solution—then solve.
Revolve like a helicopter propeller—we trendsetters
If I ask you for chocolate, don't bring me vanilla.

Never ever ever.
Strong ties never sever.
Forever clever—wolves in my circle down for whatever-ever.
Who worried about the weather? I'm looking for the clouds.
Somebody tell lightning, we can spark it up right now.

I bring pain to the rain—
Maintain a waterproof mic.
Drop a punch line on sunshine,
And push the moon out of the night.
Yeah, I'm nice like that—
But there's purpose to chase with this poetry.
Beneath the surface, there's a lower key—
Deep bass with this poetry.

Now take off that mask,
Go face-to-face with this poetry.
Serving truth on a platter—
Black history won't be erased with this poetry.

Chance-taker,
Living on faith even when it hurts.
Had to jump off the cliff
Just to prove to ya'll my wings really work.
And what do I see from the sky, looking down?
Crash dummies—smashed and splattered all over the ground.
Why put on a dog collar simply for a dollar?
Holler if you hear me—if not, don't even bother.

"Father, forgive me,"
Were the last words the killer spoke.
Laughed when he let off—
Like killing blacks folks was a joke.

Stay woke. Watch the wicked.
There's a target on your back
Consciousness under attack—
You can't even argue with none of that.

Spirit-led, ink-fed, poetically possessed.
Baraka in my bloodstream, Shaka in my chest.
If I torch the microphone, I'm sure the ashes will attest—
This ain't performance poetry...
It's a Poet's protest.

SCORPIO VOICE

I know...
Applause can be intoxicating.
Performing can feel like flying.
But a Scorpio poet knows—
the show don't end when the mic cuts off.

You still gotta perform at home,
when your family's the only audience.
When your kids are watching to see
if the fire in your poems
matches the fire in your actions.

Yeah, my words are powerful...
But words alone can't stop bullets.
Can't end racism.
Can't dismantle hate.

So I spit truth onstage,
then I live it offstage.
I show my grandson what resistance looks like
in everyday choices—
how to walk like your life matters
even when the world tells you it don't.

That's the real performance.
And it's the only one that can't afford to flop.

Now brace yourself.
Let's go Eye to I.

EYE TO I

Into the mirror, I stare.
And who is there?
I.
Two dark brown eyes looking right back at
I.
But I am who... and who am I?
My reflection replies:
You are L – A – R – R – Y.

But who is L – A – R – R – Y?
Well... if you have a moment,
Please allow me the opportunity
To introduce you to I.

Through my pupils, I view I
As more than a cool guy.
I'm an honest and true guy.
A let-it-do-what-it-do guy.
I'm fly, but not too fly.
I might rock a new tie—
A blue tie, a bow tie,
A dress shirt with no tie.

Truth be told,
If the spirit hits I just right—then I just might
Strike a pose, disrobe,
And start running through this place with no clothes,
Singing African style:
"Kumbaya, my Lord... Kumbaya."

But even if I do, I
Would only be revealing a small reflection of I.
A very tiny selection of I.
A microscopic section of he who is I.
Too complex to be simplified.
Deep-thought-provoking each time
Someone's tongue dares to mention I.

So if intervention is your intention,
That will not be necessary today for I.
See, my people and I
Have been dealing with complex situations
Since the day the first slave ship arrived.

Like that time I looked into
My grandson's young and questioning eyes.
He spoke not a word, but still...
I knew the silent question he was posing to I.
His little brown eyes looked up and he asked:

"Oh Papa, why? Papa, why?
Why do they hate I?
What horrible thing have I ever done,
To make them want to eliminate I?
Oh Papa, why? Papa, why?
Do you even have an answer for I?
What is the underlying reason
That some people are so evil
That even the mere color of my skin
Is enough to make them genuinely hate I?"

And as a tear escaped my eye,
I formulated a reply.
I said—

"The devil in disguise

Has never been a surprise to I.

See, I've been speaking to the Most High,

And He's promised me

That you and your generation are destined to survive.

So the bullets they shoot at you

Will always be intercepted—by I.

And the hateful words they spew at you

Will always be rejected—by I.

And the lies they tell to you

Will always be corrected—by I.

So until the day that I'm called to lay in my grave...

Understand, grandson:

You...

Will always be protected—

By I."

SCORPIO VOICE - WHAT POISON COULDN'T KILL

So, you've made it this far. Through the sting, the sorrow, the storm. I've watched you flinch, fight, and falter—but never fall. Now, we arrive at the edge of everything: the place where endings become origins.

This is not survival. This is resurrection.

Here, we confront the truth that tried to break us, the betrayals that burned us, and the poison that pulsed through our veins. But transformation is not reserved for the few; it's a path open to all who dare to walk it. We transmute venom into vitality, scars into symbols of strength.

In these pages, you'll witness the alchemy of agony into awakening, the metamorphosis of pain into power. This is where we rise, not despite what tried to destroy us, but because of it.

So, take a breath. Shed your old skin. Step into the fire, not to burn, but to blaze anew.

Now turn the page...
*and explore rebirth in the section we call **What Poison Couldn't Kill.***

WHAT POISON COULDN'T KILL

(REBIRTH)

I CALLED HEAVEN LAST NIGHT
(And My Mother Picked up)

I called Heaven last night,
And my mother picked up.
She said, "I miss you, my son—
And I'm sending my love.
I'm sending my light.
Let it shine at your feet.
For each step that you take
Will be guided by me."

I said, "Mother, I'm troubled.
I don't understand.
There's a cloud of confusion
Cast over this land.
Tremendous temptation
To walk in the dark...
But I know how you raised me—
I follow my heart.

And my heart beats only
To the rhythm of love...
To the drumbeat of justice,
When it's really just us.
Can I trust the protection
God promised to me?
I'm surrounded by evil.
It's following me.

As I step through the valley
With death in the shadow,
I'm asking you, Mom—
Will I live through this battle?"

My mother said,
"Son, everything's in your favor.
For you have the blessing
Of Alpha Omega.
There are questions in life...
But the answers can save you.
So always acknowledge
The grace that God gave you."

I called Heaven last night,
And my mother picked up.
She said, "I'm with your little brother—
And we both send our love."

I said, "I missed the two of you...
And I love you so much.
But these struggles on Earth
Have been tearing me up.

I'm worried about wifey
In this wicked land...
Concerned for my daughters,
And both of my grands.

Can you please talk to God—
Ask Him what is His plan?
'Cause the devil is present
With blood on his hands."

She said, "I've seen your progression.
I've watched what you've done.
In each generation,
There's always THAT one...
And you are THAT one.
Your spirit is true.
The family's intact—
Because you are the glue.

You have poured into many.
God knows what you do.
But when your cup is empty...
Who pours into you?"

I said, "My woman, my children,
My family and friends."
She said, "Son, that's God's plan—
He has blessed you with them."

And suddenly the light bulb
Switched on in my head.
Now...
I will not complain.
I'll be grateful instead.

I called Heaven last night,
And thank God—
My mother picked up.

ASHES DON'T DROWN

My mind is a stage,
And my eyes are the curtains—
When I open them wide,
You will witness my burdens.

Back bent,
Because I've been forced to **carry boulders...**
Have you ever seen a man
With the moon upon his shoulders?

Monsoon of emotions—
I was born to break barriers.
Thoughts deep as the ocean.
Storms? Never been scarier.

But still... I have risen
Beyond clouds of doubt.
Believe in yourself.
Don't let your fire die out.

Come around those with wisdom,
And learn a few things.
Live your life like a flame,
And burn a few things.

Bridges, for example—
Not all should be crossed.
Negativity on that side
Might throw your balance off.

Stay aligned with your purpose.
Yourself, you must trust.
Dirt kicked up in the air
Is still nothing but dust.

In other words—don't be fooled
By these fools and their lies.
Full of foolery, they come,
With their foolish alibis.

To the skies, we take off—
Leave that nonsense below.
Like rain, we water flowers,
And watch as they grow.

Like pain, we deal with ours,
And heal from our soul.
Maintain that inner fire...
Spit flames as we flow.

Oh. You didn't know?
Ashes don't drown.

SCORPIO VOICE

You made it through the fire, huh?

You smell like smoke—but you're still standing.
That's how I know you're ready.

See, I don't hand out healing like a pastor with a mic.
I don't sell hope in sweet little bottles with twist-off tops.
I bring the truth.

And here's the truth:

You don't rise clean.
You don't rise perfect.
You rise burned—but burning still.

You rise with scars that whisper your survival.
You rise dragging the names of every person who doubted you,
and every version of yourself you had to bury.

I've watched you crawl through broken glass for peace.
Now I dare you to walk forward like it's already yours.

The world still wants to tell you who you are.
But I've seen the real you...

Now go back and claim yourself.

REMEMBER WHO YOU ARE

(Don't You Dare Die Quietly)

When they set your dreams on fire,
You better fist-fight with the flames.
Choke the life out of the rising smoke,
Brush the ashes off of Scorpio's name.

When they submerge your hope in water,
Be a warrior and wrestle with waves.
Backstroke through your feelings of doubt,
'Cause that's how a Scorpio behaves.

When they toss your faith to the wind,
Be a cloud and catch hold of the breeze.
In due time, you'll inherit the sky,
'Cause that's what a Scorpio believes.

When they block your sun with the moon,
Be a shadow and thrive in the dark.
When you rise, they meet their demise,
Nothing eclipses a Scorpio's heart.

Don't give up now—you've come too far.
Scorpio Man—remember who you are.
Victory's yours. You are the ultimate star.
Scorpio Man—remember who you are.

MERCY

(The Voice of God Rained Down on Her)

Last night...
You gathered your wishes and threw them at a star.
And though you missed your target...
You hit the moon—which crumbled into letters that spelled out:
"God is with you wherever you are."

How are you tonight? Is life treating you right?
Is what you have with him even half a fraction
Of the beautiful blessings I can bestow upon you in just one night?

You've prayed for wings... for the ability to take flight.
So I will let **Love** lift your spirit on the winds of romance
And send you soaring to magnificent heights.

For the higher you fly, the more spectacular the view.
And the better the view, the more likely your eyes
Come to land on a **Scorpio man**,
Who will treasure you for the treasure that is you.

He'll find it a pleasure to pursue you—
In his dreams *and* in real life.
That man you're with?
He's hesitant to make you his girl...
But the Scorpio man won't hesitate to make you his **wife**.

It's been more than a moment,
But don't you ever forget—
How you told Me...
He tends to talk to you with his fist.
How you told Me...
His knuckles were the last thing you kissed.

You are **My** child.
And I never created you to be living in a nightmare such as this.

The truth?
That man holds hatred for himself.
So if **he** does not love **he**,
How can **he** love someone else?
And if **he** does not love **Me**, the G-O-D...
Find someone else.

Now...
What is this incredible sense of hesitation I sense in you, My child?
What will it take to convince you that these words I speak...
are true, My child?

It's true—you are incredible.
And you are kind.
But let not your forgiving nature
Condemn you to stay with a man
Who doesn't know whether he wants **you... or a bottle of wine.**

Time is of the essence—tick... tock...
Time for you to decide
Whether you will love him... or love him not.

But while you're in the midst of being judgmental,
Please do not forget to also be **self**-judgmental.

For you have skeletons of your own.
And your closet?
I've often looked into.

I've seen the bones of jealousy, greed, and lust.
I've seen the bones of hatred, envy, and mistrust.
I've seen chicken bones, rib bones, neck bones...
And on your worst day,
I think I even saw a Tyrannosaurus Rex bone.

But nevertheless...
It's time for you to confess.

Have you always told Me when you've done wrong?
No.

So it should be easy for you to see...
You and that no-good man?
Are **nothing** without **My mercy**.

Now go...
Find you a Scorpio man.

ANIMALISTIC
(I Don't Walk as Man)

I'm rattlesnake in battle, wait.
I'm crocodile down by the lake.
I'm tiger, run, you can't escape,
Or maybe I'm gorilla, Ape.

I'm zebra, striped in black-and-white.
I'm cheetah, sprint, I quickly strike.
I'm eagle, soar, see me in flight.
Hyena, bite, I hunt at night.

I'm lion, Simba, jungle King.
I'm jaguar black, mystique I bring.
Orangutan, in trees, I swing.
I'm Scorpio, of course, I sting.

I'm wolf in woods, I lead the pack.
I'm leopard, lurking, sneak attack.
Coyote, creeping, watch your back.
I'm hippo, hungry, who's the snack?

I'm bumblebee, my buzz, unique.
I'm gopher, dig, my tunnel's deep.
I'm kangaroo, hop, fifteen feet.
I'm shark, and you're my dinner treat.

I'm elephant, big body, large.
I'm buffalo, stampede, I charge.
I'm raccoon, rough, I run this yard.
I'm rhino, tough, my horn stays hard.

I'm human, cursed, took God for granted.
Homosapien, earthbound, stranded.
Mankind, life ain't like I planned it.
Man messed up this whole damn planet.

Man, the animal—soulless, greed.
Poisoned the air, cut down the trees.
Burned the sky, then blamed the sun.
Built his kingdom, grabbed his gun.

Man messed up this whole damn planet—
Took paradise, and could not manage.
I shed my skin, returned to land...
I am beast, now—
I don't walk as man.

SCORPIO VOICE

OK, OK—I'll admit it.
That did get a bit wild.
But Scorpio has always been
More jungle animal than house pet.

And to be real—
You'd better have a little beast in you
if you want to survive in this wicked world.

But this ain't about rage.
This is rebirth.
We're talking what poison couldn't kill.
And the one thing that never dies...

Is the memory of the woman who birthed the Scorpio man.

Illness took her body.
But her spirit?
She lives on...
*as my beautiful **Black Butterfly.***

SCENE:
Backyard - Warm Satuday Morning - 11:11 am

A man in shorts reclines in a patio chair, scrolling his phone.
He pauses on a photo of his mother—
Gone, but never distant.

His chest tightens. Eyes sting.
Then—
A black butterfly lands on his hand.

He exhales.
Smiles.
"Good morning, Mama," he whispers.

BLACK BUTTERFLY
(Such a Painful Goodbye)

Oh my, Black Butterfly—metamorphosis, done.
Wings spread wide. Destination: the sun.
Altitude high, clouds measure the height—
A dream in the daytime, a miracle at night.

Much more than majestic, so flawless in flight...
Heavenly ascension. Find peace in the light.
Far from ordinary—no stereotype.
My heart fell apart at your burial site.

I cried when you died—such a painful goodbye.
But now you appear as my Black Butterfly.
Now you appear as my Black Butterfly.
Mother, now you appear as my Black Butterfly.

Oh my, Black Butterfly—flower's best friend.
Soul of the sky. Newlywed to the wind.
A glorious glide. Eloquent when you soar.
A bride to the breeze. Caterpillar no more.

Behold the true beauty. Transformative trance.
Amazing to witness a butterfly dance.
Hypnotizing. Fly high—fast fluttering wings.
Blessed are the eyes that discover you, Queen.

I cried when you died—such a painful goodbye.
But now you appear as my Black Butterfly.
Now you appear as my Black Butterfly.
Mother, now you appear as my Black Butterfly.

SCORPIO VOICE

So what now?
You thought rebirth was just about survival?
Nah.
It's about radiance.
It's about looking death in the eye, brushing off the ashes,
and still having the audacity to glow.

Let me tell you something about being melanated—
It's not just pigment, it's power.
It's ancestral memory, soul-deep rhythm,
and a sun-kissed crown that don't come off in the storm.

We've watched too many kings fall,
buried too many queens—
and still we rise.
Not out of tradition,
but out of divine design.

You can't kill what was kissed by creation.
You can't erase what was written in star-dust and struggle.

We are the aftershock.
The second breath.
The final bloom.

And when the light hits us just right—
we don't shine...

we blaze.

GOD BLESS THE MELANATED

Transformation to man from the prodigy son.
Elevation at hand—haters, we all have some.

Him talk too **Black**—the boujee people mumble.
Him walk too **Black**—**gorilla stomp in the jungle**.

I wonder what the wicked really want when they police me?
Do they see me as a king or Rodney King—kick, stomp, and beat me?
Completely incog-negro, move in silence, dance discreetly.
A glorious day soon come—God will appear in His dashiki.
Peace seekers tell me, "Pray," but we the lions who keep roaring.
Goliath in our way—we fear no giants; we destroy them.
Tired of praying for our freedom—no offense to any Reverend—
But the day I die on Earth, the revolution gonna start in Heaven.

How do I know I'll go to Heaven?
Elohim, He wrote the sequel.
I've gotta be part of the chosen—
The way these demons come at my people:
Attack after attack... attack after attack.
Thought I was grounded
Till these angel wings just grew up out my back.

I flap my feathers till I fly—way up high where the falcons be.
I dream to be Dr. King without being killed upon that balcony.
I flex to be the next X without my skinful, trying to Malcolm me.
See, I am my brother's keeper—
That's why the Reaper keeps coming after me.

And what do I hope to see
When I reach the pearly gates?
George Floyd doing well,
And he's breathing really great.
Sandra Bland in her car—
She's just cruising right along.
Trayvon Martin, eating Skittles,
And he safely makes it home.
Tamir Rice in that park—
And he's playing like the rest.
Breonna Taylor in her bed
Without the bullets in her flesh.

God bless the melanated—
Highly favored and celebrated.
And if we want a better day...
Black love will create it.

Let's turn jails into Yale.
Prisons into Princeton.
Leave that fried food alone
So you don't die of hypertension.
Let's turn the streets into Spelman.
The hood into Howard.
Kings are ready to fight;
These queens ain't raising any cowards.

More power to the people
Who were taken from the Motherland.
Consider yourself woke—
Then do the work and wake another man.

I love you, my brother man.
I trust you, my brother man.
No matter what they say…
I'm gonna hug you, my brother man.

I love you, my sister queen.
I trust you, my sister queen.
No matter what we go through…
I'm gonna hug you, my sister queen.

Our dreams are intertwined.
You plus me equals divine.
Take your seat upon that throne—
I'll shine your crown if you don't mind.
I'll stay around if you don't mind.
I'll hold you down if you don't mind.
Teach you to swim—won't let you drown.
Erase your frown if you don't mind.

God bless the melanated—
Highly favored and celebrated.
And if we want a better day…
Black love will create it.

AFRO-ALIEN

(Rebirth of a Scorpio Seed)

I am Afro-Alien, original Black being from above—
Beyond the bounds of your logic, I am rhythm, I am love.
Far superior to mankind, my kind comes from afar,
Speaking Swahili on spaceships, beating drums upon a star.

They told me I was too much—too Black to be sane,
So I left their dimension and rewired my brain.
They buried me broken, too loud, too strong...
But I resurrected in silence, where ancestors belong.

Now I build where the clouds form nations of peace,
And dance where the pain of my people can cease.
Chocolate City awaits like paradise in the sky,
Ascension to places most thought were too high
I reach for dimensions mere mortals deny—
It's war of attrition: you live or you die.

And who am I?
The universal verse spitter, reversing the curse,
Dispersing the worst of humanity, unearthing its thirst.
Birth of a new nation, patiently waiting to form,
Anticipation of elevation—my pen creates the storm.

Warm, in fact—Fahrenheit at levels too high.
Devils cry when an angel's preparing to fly.
Multiply prosperity, let poverty fall,
Be a champion of charity, and still stand tall.

Long live lyrical legends—put Larry on that.
Booked a stage in the clouds—I'm getting married on that.
Spotlight in my direction, am I shining enough?
If I never see progression, am I grinding enough?

Find it rough in the wild, where the owls are in flight,
Nocturnally hunting, with clear vision at night.
Indecision replaced with precision—I strike,
It's a mid-air collision between me and my mic.

Rhymes fall like meteorites—run for cover,
Or live in the light of this alien brother.
Negativity left on land when I lifted,
Agility, intelligence—damn, I'm so gifted.

Prolific, uplifted, reborn from the fire,
My zodiac code is a live amplifier.
Scorpio sent me—tattooed on my fate,
To sting with the truth and resurrect what they hate.
I just rose from the ashes, expanded my wings...
Afro-Alien, Scorpio, Galaxy King!

SCORPIO VOICE - THE LAST WORD

So... you made it.
Through love that burned.
Through life that bled.
Through liberation that demanded your soul.
And now, here you are—rebirthed.

You didn't get here alone.

I led you.

I walked you through the venom and devotion.
I dragged you through the weight of water.
I marched you straight into the fire for your freedom.
And I stood watch as you rose from the ashes.

That was me.
Scorpio.

Not your savior.
Your mirror.
Your shadow.
Your truth.

You were never meant to come out the same.

Now you've seen what lives beneath the skin.
Felt what burns behind the eyes.
Heard what silence sounds like
Before the scream.

And me?

I'm not walking you any further.

You've got wings now.

Fly.

Acknowledgments

This book didn't just happen—it was built, brick by brick, by the hands and hearts of the people in my life.

To my wife, **Diane**, thank you for the patience, encouragement, and steady presence that kept me balanced while I wrestled with every page. To my daughters, **Jasmin** and **Khyra**, and my grandchildren, **Terrell** and **Ta'Mia**—thank you for reminding me why my words must matter.

To my parents—my mother, **Jacqueline**, whose unwavering belief in me still guides me from Heaven, and my father, **Watani**, whose strength and wisdom keep me grounded—you gave me both roots and wings.

To my brother, **Sham**—your absence is felt, but your spirit is stitched into every performance, every poem, every breath of this book.

To **Andrea Lee**, thank you for a friendship and business partnership that has been both inspiring and transformative. To **Lynette**, **Lynetta**, **Big Rob**, **Lige**, **Jan Land**, **Tracy (TJ)**, and **Delicia Defour**—thank you for showing up in ways that mattered most.

To my **Creative Love Network** family—this isn't just an organization, it's a movement. We've created something rare, and the best chapters are still ahead.

And to the **poetry community**—your stages, your open mics, your encouragement, your poems and your energy have been fuel for my journey. This book may carry my name, but its heartbeat belongs to all of you.

About the Author

Larry Love, a South Los Angeles native born on October 25 in the heart of Scorpio Season, is a poet, spoken word artist, and storyteller whose work fuses raw emotion, cultural truth, and cinematic imagery. Known for his commanding stage presence and unflinching delivery, he channels the mystique and intensity of Scorpio energy into every performance. As founder and CEO of **Creative Love Network**, where poetry production meets personal transformation, Larry has written, directed, and produced acclaimed spoken word and musical stage plays that have stirred hearts and provoked thought on every stage they've touched. His voice has carried from the haunting echoes of Alcatraz to the sunlit shores of the Bahamas, and into classrooms and universities, where his words spark reflection, dialogue, and change on love, life, and justice.

A youth mentor, husband, and father, Larry's artistry is rooted in love, legacy, and liberation—deeply informed by the Black experience and the ongoing fight for equity. His performances and writings confront the beauty and brutality of life, leaving audiences moved and challenged in equal measure. With Scorpio Man: Black Roses & Revolution, he invites readers into a world where passion stings, truth cuts, and resilience blooms like a black rose through concrete.

About the Publisher

Creative Love Network is a Southern California based poetry and live performance organization that utilizes spoken word and the arts as a means to entertain audiences, deliver targeted messages and positively impact communities. The company is rooted in the understanding that words, whether they are spoken, sang, read or heard, have the power to change lives and shape the world.

The Creative Love Network's Four Pillars—foundational company principles and affirmations—are:

Love:
I will love myself and others, and I will do things out of love.

Organize:
I will organize my life, and I will seek order over chaos.

Value:
I will value the whole of me, and I will see the value in others.

Evolve:
I will evolve into a better me,
and I will always work to improve as a person.

**I believe that when I LOVE, ORGANIZE, VALUE & EVOLVE,
I am doing my part to make the world a better place.**

L.O.V.E.
creativelovenetwork.com

CREATIVE LOVE

NETWORK